Uniform*ar*

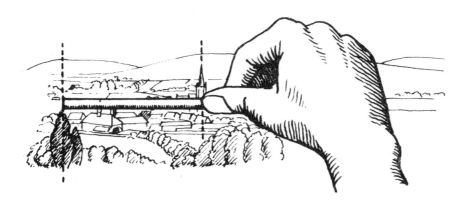

Twentyeighteen

Uniformannual

We've deferred the next issue of the quarterly *Uniformagazine* (no.11) for the moment in order to publish this first *Uniformannual*. Tapping into some idea of what an annual might be, or at least look like, it is a hardback with printed paper over boards, and uncoated stock, good for type and illustrations but not so good for reproducing photographs (although there are plenty of half-tones). There are 124 pages printed in black and the folded sections have been notched and glued. The blue 'cloth' cover is printed in colour and laminated.

The contributions are from some of the writers, artists, and researchers that we have worked with, or are currently working with, on books and in *Uniformagazine*. The choice of the content has been *ad hoc*, offering the possibility to select and gather some extensive idea of subject and association.

Short biographies of the twenty-four contributors are included at the back, and full details of our titles can be found on the website: *uniformbooks.co.uk*. All of our books and back issues of *Uniformagazine* can be ordered direct from us, as well as through online booksellers and independent bookshops. Keep updated about future projects by following us on Twitter: @Uniformbooks.

Contents

Chimney Days

Tim Staples

It's ten years ago that I began activities on Leigh Hill: repointing the remains of an old brick chimney (see 'Local History Sculpture' *Uniformagazine* no.1, Autumn 2014). Annual visits, in blocks of twenty-eight days or so, are made during the warmer months, although personal circumstances in 2013 and 2015 conspired against continuous attendance. This adds up to about eight months in total and questions have begun to be asked along the lines of: "when are you going to finish it?" or "what are you doing up there?" To a degree, that well-worn expression, "the devil is in the detail" holds true and this article presents an opportunity to check on progress.

By 2011 the rebuild of the upper ten courses of brickwork had been completed, including coping stones made from old roofing slates (above). These were necessary to prevent the penetration of rainwater down through the mortar joints in what is probably the most vulnerable part of the structure in terms of weathering. These slates are barely visible, even when in close proximity to the chimney; in fact a ladder is required to see them in their entirety. As a rule, stone or concrete coping stones are a minimum of two inches thick, so the use of these slates enabled the overall visual form of the structure to remain faithful to my first encounter with it. Throughout the meanderings of the whole undertaking, this has been an ever-present guiding principle, with only minor adjustments being considered. The delicate balance between the demands of practicality and the imperative of holding true to a vision.

That same year, prior to packing up for the season in early October, a major change was forced on the site, resulting in the creation of a fenced-in compound. This encompassed the area between the chimney in the north and a group of ash trees to the south, in all an area measuring approximately seventy by forty feet. The decision was precipitated as a means of protection from the imminent arrival of cattle in the field and was suggested by the farmer's son. Reluctant to go ahead, I didn't want the chimney or indeed myself when onsite, to be quite literally framed! Furthermore, being fenced off and separated from the rest of the field carried with it the stamp of officialdom. I feared, to coin a phrase, being "English Heritaged"! But needs must and in this instance matters of practicality were in the ascendancy.

For the uninitiated, cattle can cause considerable damage to anything in their way. They churn up the ground turning it into a morass of mud anywhere they gather; like gateways, feeding stations or places where they find something to rub themselves against—like an old chimney for example or indeed a campervan. Sheep do the same but without as much collateral damage. Under the circumstances it was the right thing to do but that feeling of being fenced-in took a long while to get used to and completely changed the experience of being there. Pre-compound life had felt comparable to what I imagined it might be like to inhabit one of Thomas Bewick's tailpieces.

Eventually, when the practical work is all done, the fence will be taken down and the site returned from a framed, 'look I'm special', delineated compound, to how it used to be—something analogous to a vignette. Seen from the road, a cluster of ash trees, a brick structure set behind with its adjacent birch tree; isolated in a field of grassland but close enough to each other to be read as belonging together.

As it turned out, the cattle were only in the field during that winter and haven't been back since. However, the possibility of their return hovered in the background, prompting, in 2014, a new phase of work. Having spent so much time and energy on the upper parts, now it was the turn of the base to receive some attention. Digging out the hearth revealed just how flimsy the foundations actually were. This wasn't surprising and once dug out it was backfilled with a mixture of concrete bulked out with large stones. The final stage was to finish it with flat pieces of chert, level with the bottom of the first course of bricks and then pointed-in. Also included was a central drainage hole, filled with white pebbles from the soil that had been dug out (opposite, far right).

In 2016–17 an identical procedure was repeated all the way around the chimney to form a pavement two foot six wide. However, the finished height of this was made both lower than that of the hearth and also inclined away from the structure to facilitate drainage. Cattle can now come and do their worst. However, for the moment it will be left as it is, until all the pointing is complete. The final act will be to cover the pavement with soil, just shy of the foundation edging stones, and then reseed. Once grass and weeds have regrown, my annual presence for passers by will soon fade into obscurity. And that's just how it should be.

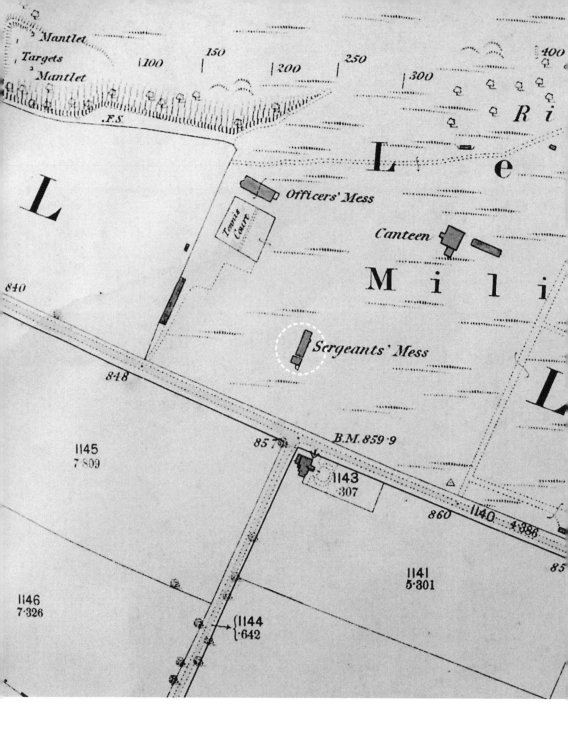

The chimney is all that remains of the Sergeants' Mess: a building constructed from wood and corrugated iron in 1884 and part of a now lost camp used by the Somerset Militia between 1873–98. At some point after 1947, the building disappeared (local legend has it in the 1980s) leaving the chimney vulnerable to the ravages of the elements and human intervention, on a site that is particularly exposed.

Set on a plateau over 850 feet above sea level at the edge of the Blackdown Hills, its north-facing border is defined by an escarpment. Prior to enclosure in the nineteenth century, the land here formed part of Pitminster Common, although today public access is not permitted as the area is privately owned farmland and there are no public rights of way.

Geography

Gertrude Stein

As geography return to geography, return geography. Geography. Comes next. Geography. Comes. Comes geography.

As geography returns to geography comes next geography. Comes. Comes geography.

Geography as nice. Comes next geography. Geography as nice comes next geography comes geography.

Geographically, geographical. Geographically to place, geographically in case in case of it.

Looking up under fairly see fairly looking up under as to movement. The movement described. Sucked in met in, met in set in, sent in sent out sucked in sucked out.

An interval.

If it needs if it needs if it needs to do not move, do not move, do not touch, do not touch, do not if it needs to if it needs. That is what she is looking for. Less. Less threads fairly nearly and geography and water. Descriptive emotion. As it can be.

He was terribly deceived about the Jews about Napoleon and about everything else.

If you do not know the meaning of such things do not use them. That is all. Such phrases.

More geography, more than, more geography. Which bird what bird more geography. Than geography.

Geography pleases me that is to say not easily. Beside it is decided. Geographically quickly. Not geographically but geography.

Geographically not inland not an island and the sea. It is what it is good for to sit by it to eat and to go away. Every time then to come again and so there is an interruption.

Plentifully simply. Napoleon is dimply.

If the water comes into the water if the water as it comes into the water makes as much more as it should can snow melt. If the water as it should does snow melt and could it as it has melted could it melt and does it and does it melt and should it, should it melt and would it melt and does it melt and will it melt and can it and does it melt. As water. I often think about seasonable.

Waterfully when the water waterfully when the water comes to soften when the water comes and to soften when the water and to soften, waterfully and to soften, when the water and to soften, not wetter. When the water and to soften I know noises. As to noises. When the water and to soften as to water as to soften I know I know noises. I have secretly wished altogether. One two three altogether.

Geographically and inundated, geography and inundated, not inundated.

He says that the rain, he says that for rain he says that for snow he says, he says that the rain he says that the snow he says that the rain that the snow he says that is rain he says that is snow he says it is rain he says it is rain he says that it is snow he says it is snow.

He says it is snow.

Paper very well. Paper and water and very well. Paper and water and very well and paper and water and very well and paper and very well and water. Paper and water very well.

Naturally and water colour the colour of water and naturally. Very naturally the colour and very naturally. It is the best yet.

When this you see remember for me remember it for me if you can.

Once again as we can, once again and as we can, once again and as we can and once again and once again and as we can and can.

New to you. New to us. New. I knew. This is a very interesting thing to ask. To ask if it is new if it is new to you. It is a very interesting thing to ask.

It is a very interesting thing to know. That is a very interesting thing to know. Do you know whether it is new whether it is as new whether it is new to you. It is a very interesting thing to know that it is as new as it is to you.

I stands for Iowa and Italy. M stands for Mexico and Monte Carlo. G stands for geographic and geographically. B stands for best and most. It is very nearly decided.

Immeasurably. Immeasurably and frequently. Frequently and invariably. Invariably and contentedly. Contentedly and indefatigably. Indefatigably and circumstances. Circumstances and circumstantially. Initiative and reference. In reference to it. It needs to be added to, in addition. Additionally as in reduction. In geography and in geography.

As it might be said to be as it might be said to be.

As at this was was was as it was was was as it was.

Not to be outdone in kindness.

Can you tell can you really tell it from here, can you really tell it can you tell it can you tell from here. From here to there and from there to there. Put it there. Is he still there.

If to say it if to see it if to say it. If to say it. The point of it, the point is this, that point at that point and twenty at that point and not twenty if you see and if you say it. If you say it and if you see it. As at that point and twenty. Twenty twenty a new figure. And a new finger. As a direction as in a direction. And so in whistling incorrectly. Very near and very near and very nearly and very nearly and very near it was a very near thing, very near to it. Amuse yourself. Vastly.

So much and as much. Much and as much, much and so much. Much and very much, very much and as much. Thank you for it.

Pardon me plainly pardon me. In this and hear. Here. Here at once. Not exactly angry. How exactly angry. Fed as to wheat. Seated by me. Sat and that. If to please. Instead.

Cochin chine as Cochin China Tuesday. What is my delight.

No not that and no not that. And designs and the post, post mark. As dark. We know how to feel British. Saving stamps. Excuse me.

To make no allusion to anybody. Spread as glass is, glass is spread and so are colours, colours and pretty ways.

Able and Mabel. Mabel and able.

As outing. As an outing can it please me.

Leave and leave and leave relieve and relieve and relieve, candy as everywhere, but it is if it is, have happen. I touched it.

As through.

Shipping not shipping shipping not shipping, shipping as shipping shipping in shipping in shipping it. In shipping it as easily. Famous as a sire.

Notably notably reading.

Fasten as lengthily. As one day.

Smell sweetly. Industriously and indeed. It is apt to be.

Is it very apt to be explained.

I know how to wait. This is a joke. It is a pun.

Feasibly. A market as market to market.

In standing in plenty of ways, attending to it in plenty of ways, as opera glasses in plenty of ways as raining and in plenty of ways, hard as a pear run in the way, ran in this way. Ran away. I know the exact size and shape and surface and use and distance. To place it with them.

Any many many any any many many any any many many any any many many any. Any one.

Geography includes inhabitants and vessels.

Plenty of planning.

Geographically not at all.

September 1923

Opposite: Detail of a photograph by Man Ray, 'Gertrude Stein in her salon, writing', c.1920.

Michael

Erica Van Horn

Monday, 7 August
An elderly robin has become a friend. He stays nearby whenever we are outside.
Mostly he sits on the back of the chair where one of us is sitting. Then he moves to
sit with the other one of us. He hops along the tabletop. His head and wing feathers
and his red breast are scruffy looking. That is how we know he is not young.
His scruffiness is what makes him distinctive. It does not matter which table
we are sitting at or whether we are drinking tea or coffee. He seems to like the
companionship. Or maybe it is the sound of our voices.

Wednesday, 9 August
The robin has a name now. He is Michael. He joins us by the back door and he sits
with us at the large table over by the fence. Wherever we are out of doors, Michael
appears and is committed to Staying Near. He sat on a branch while I picked
raspberries. He came into the kitchen and rested on the windowsill while we were
preparing food and cleaning up. He jumps when there are sudden movements or
loud noises but he seems to enjoy quiet words or nonsense syllables babbled softly
in his direction. We are not getting too much done because we are constantly
popping in and out or looking out a window to see where Michael is. We crumbled
up crackers on the table for him. There is water for him to drink. He came with me
as I went all around the tree and up the stone steps squeezing figs to test them for
ripeness. He appears to pay careful attention to every single thing that is done out
of doors.

Friday, 11 August
Michael was late arriving this morning. Every day he has been waiting on the table
outside the kitchen before we are even up. He was doing the morning waiting for
a long while before we realised that it was the same bird out waiting out there
every morning. Today there was no sign of him until noon. We were worried about
his leg. We are still worried about his leg. One leg is now at a wonky angle. The
displacing of the leg happened some time yesterday. A bigger fatter stronger robin
had been rushing onto the table and chasing Michael away each time he was there.
That was when we realised that Michael is not an old bird as we first thought. He
is a very young bird. The older robin who was pushing him out of the way had
seniority. At the end of the afternoon we saw that Michael's left leg was sticking
out at a right angle. He kept falling over while trying to eat crumbs. We think he
flew at a window and knocked himself down onto the ground. But we wonder if
the older fat robin chased him and frightened him and forced him into the window
or the wall of the house. It must be the impact with the ground that damaged his

15

leg. We were happy to see him back today but we are worried about the leg. We are worried and we have no idea what to do about it.

Tuesday, 15 August
Michael is here to greet us. Michael is here to greet us whenever we return to the house. It does not matter if we are coming back from ten minutes away or from three days away. He arrives and hovers close and comes indoors and generally lets us know that he is glad to be nearby. I have now been told that it is normal for young robins to adopt people. I thought we were special and that Michael was special. I still think he is special. It is just that it is not such an unusual thing to have him want to be with us. I do not mind that. Michael flies away when the other robin comes to frighten him but nothing we do frightens him. He has graduated to sitting on Simon's shoulder now. He has not sat upon me yet but he is happy to sit very close to me.

Friday, 18 August
Michael sat on a low leaf while I collected figs. His leg looks much better. He still favours it, but it no longer sticks out at that terrible angle. He sat on leaves or on large stones while I picked raspberries. He has no interest in eating fruit. Maybe robins do not eat fruit or maybe he is just too young to know that he might love it.

Saturday, 26 August
This morning Michael is sitting on the table while he eats his crumbs. He sits on the table the way a mother bird sits on her nest. His left leg has gone off into the same uncomfortable looking angle it was at a week ago. We thought it was fully healed. Now it looks like a bit of wire hanging off his body. It does not look like a leg. It is worrying. When he stands on the dish taking sips of water, he can hardly stop himself from falling into the water. Balancing on one leg is no treat. Luckily flying is no problem for him. I use a piece of Kilkenny limestone to gently smash his biscuits into small pieces. He does not fly away when I mash. He stays close waiting until I stop so that he can begin eating.

Thursday, 31 August
Michael was being badly bullied by some bigger fatter robins this morning. He walked into the kitchen so I fed him some cracker crumbs on the floor. He ate in his sitting down position in peace and quiet.

Sunday, 3 September
Michael sits on my knee. He sits on Simon's shoulder. He has not sat upon my shoulder and he has not sat upon Simon's knee. Today he sat on Maud's foot. He is completely happy to be near us and on us. Sudden movements frighten him but mostly he appears to like the sound of voices and the presence of people. He made a diving attack on some other robins who showed up and started to eat some of his

crumbs so I am less worried about him being able to survive than I was. His leg is bent but it does not stop him from flying. It does not dangle from his body in quite such a useless way as it did a few days ago.

Friday, 8 September
The winds are wild and gusty. We are being buffeted about. The sound of the wind is never not in my ears. It is always in my ears. I hear it when I am inside the house and I hear it when I am outside the house. I hear it while I sleep and while I eat. I hear it while I am thinking of other things. I am worried about Michael. I have not seen him all day. I hope he is tucked away somewhere safe and out of the wind. I think he spends a lot of time under the rosemary bush. I hope he has plenty to eat.

Monday, 11 September
The wind never stops. It never stops. It is exciting and it is completely annoying. I cannot remember how long it has been. It seems like it has been windy forever. I feel we could be blown away. We might end up in another country or at least another county. The sun has come out and in between glorious bright sunshine there are small amounts of rain. The rain falls while the sun shines. Every few minutes the day is different. Some robins have appeared around the table. They are here to eat crumbs but none of the robins are Michael. I am looking carefully at their markings and their legs which are all strong and straight. I am looking for the crooked tail feather. I am worried. I thought maybe all the robins had gone away but that is not the case. I wonder if Michael has been chased away by bigger birds or if he has been blown away by the wind or if he has been the victim of a bigger creature. Some of the robins are here. Where is Michael?

Wednesday, 13 September
I am hoping that Michael has found a new place to call his own. I do not know if the other robins chased him away. There are two robins who still stop at the table regularly. They both have fat bodies and strong straight legs. They are not Michael. I was worried about him in the wild winds but the winds have stopped now. I thought he might be sheltering but if that was the case he should be back. I have spent time in the places he used to go with me. I have picked raspberries and talked to him as if he was nearby. I hoped that if he was hiding my voice might encourage him to come out. I have done some weeding. I have sat on the kitchen bench and I have drunk tea out at the big table always hoping and hoping he might appear. I have been hoping his curiosity would make him come along to see what I was doing. Yesterday I sat on the bench in the rain under an umbrella just in case he felt the rain provided a safe time to come out of hiding. Most birds are not out in the rain. I hope wherever he is that he is happy. He might not remember our voices and our treats. The brain of a robin might not hold onto a past. Maybe the present is enough. I still look for him outside many times each day. I hope he is not dead.

English autumn mornings are often like mornings nowhere else in the world. The air is cold. The floorboards are cold. It is perhaps this coldness which

sharpens the tang of the hot cup of tea. Outside, steps on the gravel crunch a little more loudly than a month ago because of the very slight frost. There is

John Berger

Ken Worpole

I first read John Berger in the late 1960s in his occasional pieces for the weekly journal, *New Society*. They were quite unlike anything else in that sociologically-inflected but much admired magazine, often including drawings and small fragments of poetry. One short essay concluded by citing a Russian proverb—"Life is not a walk across an open field"—which I've remembered to this day. At some point *New Society* began to run extracts from a forthcoming book by Berger in collaboration with photographer Jean Mohr, *A Fortunate Man: The story of a country doctor*, which, on publication in 1967, I actually bought new. This was a rare event for a book collector on limited means as I was then. It soon became the work that, more than any other, re-shaped my imaginative life, fostering an abiding fascination with the relationship between writing and photography, as well as investigating what might be meant by the idea of a life's vocation.

With echoes of Turgenev's *Fathers and Sons*, or Georges Bernanos' *The Diary of a Country Priest*, it documented the daily round of a real-life doctor, Dr Sassall, serving a small community in rural Gloucestershire, in circumstances where for many of his patients life was something to be endured rather than enjoyed. In short, it was about

'We fell in love with it ten years ago – for the view. And I must say we've never regretted it, not even in the winter. It's so peaceful. Do you know last spring

when I was walking along the path from the village I saw something standing in the front gate. I could see it as I turned the corner by the wood. It looked like

the ethics of vocation, which as someone then training to be a teacher was becoming an important question to be asking oneself. For although I knew Berger to be a self-declared Marxist, this deeply sympathetic book celebrated the idea of vocation over and above the reductionist view of teaching and other public professions espoused by mainstream Marxist ideology.

Berger saw Dr Sassall as "a clerk of the records", a dutiful man who listened to the stories people told him about themselves and their lives, thus validating their experiences. Jean Mohr's photographs widened the scope and ambition of the book with a series of portraits of Sassall at work, but also of the landscape he traversed daily, a rural landscape that provided the background for his patients, for some the only landscape they would ever know from birth to death. For Berger, the natural world was not simply a stage set, for in *A Fortunate Man* he wrote that: "Sometimes a landscape seems to be less a setting for the life of its inhabitants than a curtain behind which their struggles, achievements and accidents take place".

He and Mohr later recalled that they had to negotiate their respective roles in the making of this book, so that what at first had been in danger of becoming a traditional text illustrated by photographs needed instead to become "a conversation, building on, rather than mirroring, one another". The effect was a complete re-invention of documentary form, with the words and the photographs independently complementing, independently challenging, but amplifying and enriching each other, a mode of working from which Jason Orton and I learned

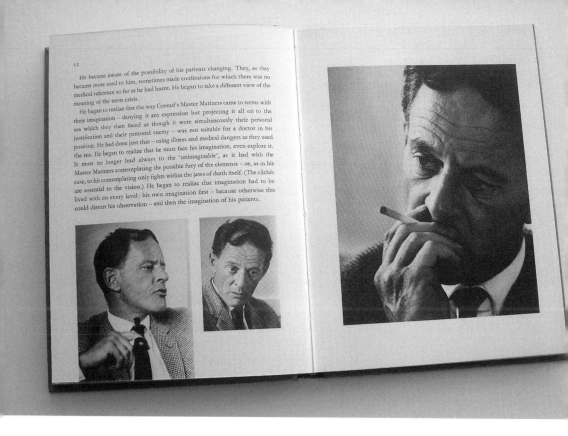

52

He became aware of the possibility of his patients changing. They, as they became more used to him, sometimes made confessions for which there was no medical reference so far as he had learnt. He began to take a different view of the meaning of the term crisis.

He began to realize that the way Conrad's Master Mariners came to terms with their imagination – denying it any expression but projecting it all on to the sea which they then faced as though it were simultaneously their personal justification and their personal enemy – was not suitable for a doctor in his position. He had done just that – using illness and medical dangers as they used the sea. He began to realize that he must face his imagination, even explore it. It must no longer lead always to the 'unimaginable', as it had with the Master Mariners contemplating the possible fury of the elements – or, as in his case, to his contemplating only fights within the jaws of death itself. (The clichés are essential to the vision.) He began to realize that imagination had to be lived with on every level: his own imagination first – because otherwise this could distort his observation – and then the imagination of his patients.

much. Berger frequently collaborated with others, perhaps most famously with Jean Mohr, but also with film-maker Mike Dibb on the TV series, 'Ways of Seeing', and painter John Christie. His life was constantly lived in conversation with others, both the living and the dead, close by and across the world.

Another two books by John Berger have a particular significance for me. His 2005 collection of stories about meetings with the dead, *Here is Where We Meet*, is one. I had thought I was somewhat eccentric in regarding the companionate dead—those people I knew who had since died—as dear to me as many of my living family and friends—but so did Berger. But there was an additional pre-occupation which Berger addressed directly—and again unusually—when he gives the dead the role of returning to the earth to repair what has been broken. (There is a long established Talmudic belief that the work of the good on earth is to repair the world). Thus he has his mother, who after dying returns to Lisbon to live her second life, where Berger meets up with her again. In one of their walks they come across a dog barking furiously. "One thing repaired changes a thousand others", insists the mother, and although the incident is traditionally expressed, the politics belong to the future. Noticing that the chain on the dog is too short to allow it reach the shade, hence its distress, she suggests that by lengthening the chain just a little the dog will find shade and stop barking. Thus the family and neighbours will become happier and start talking to each other again, and many other good things might flow from this one small act of thoughtfulness.

20

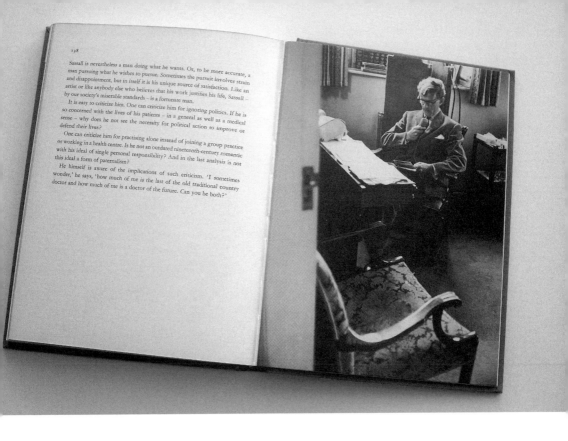

The *Red Tenda of Bologna*, with drawings by Paul Davis, published in 2007, is another favourite. It is a family story, yet again, this time of a fond uncle, long dead, whom Berger 'meets' again unexpectedly in Bologna, a city both men loved—as I do too. The red 'Tenda' are the shop blinds that distinguish many of the arcaded cafés and stores, but whose exceptional colour—and Berger was obsessed with pigmentation and its provenance—dramatised his memory of the city. The small book ranges across food, paintings, memories of the resistance, and martyrdom. On several visits some years ago Larraine Worpole and I spent days—she taking the photographs, myself taking notes—recording the many memorable tombs and public memorials, in La Certosa Cemetery, and in the city itself, for a book we did together, *Last Landscapes: the architecture of the cemetery in the West*. The memorial to the partisan resistance during the Second World War in the town square, which Berger describes in relation to a poem by Pasolini, is painfully unforgettable.

Berger's work has been incomparable in so many fields of political and cultural creativity. Sometimes the debt owed by his admirers has been obvious. The two volumes of Working Lives a group of us published in Hackney in the 1970s as part of an oral history project, mixing transcribed text with photographs, were a direct homage to Berger and Mohr's *A Seventh Man*. But his influence has been subtle and pervasive in many other ways. We shall be walking and talking with John Berger for a long time to come.

Supataps

Ian Waites

Studies on memory, such as Martin A. Conway's *Autobiographical Memory: An Introduction* (1990), generally begin with the premise that the experience of remembering is determined by the recall of events or episodes that are dominated by a particular sense of place and time. The memories of our childhood in particular are often formed by vivid, visual reference-points that are the remnants of the intense and unmediated experiences of the child. My very earliest memory is of my three year-old self being taken by my Mum and Dad to view what became our new council house in the spring of 1964. For me, that visit is dominated by one visual reference point: the sight of the large red and blue dots that were embedded in the top of the chrome taps that hung over the stainless steel kitchen sink.

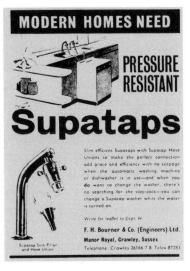

These taps had a name. They were called Supataps, and they were all the rage in the 1950s and '60s due, I suppose, to their space-age (ish) design, but mostly to the fact you could change the washer on them without having to turn off the water supply. At that time, Supataps were the modern home's tap of choice, and the adverts of the time clearly reflected that.

These days, I tend to articulate the memory of seeing those taps in terms of being transported from a monochrome nothingness into a pop art world of red and blue dots, as my family finally crossed the threshold into 'The Sixties'. But now I'm not sure how reliable the memory is, or the sentiment that I attach to it.

As we enter adulthood, the direct sensory experiences of our childhood become dulled by familiarity, and they are gradually substituted by a mode of appreciation and remembrance to the point where we become almost wholly incapable of recalling or even imagining what we saw and felt as a child. Nearly all that can we can experience has already been had. As Jorge Luis Borges once said: "Memory changes things. Every time we remember something, after the first time, we're not remembering the event, but the first memory of the event. Then the second experience of the second memory and so on".

Or, as the psychologist and author of *Pieces of Light: The New Science of Memory* (2013), Charles Fernyhough put it, "Our memories are created in the present, rather than being faithful records of the past". But if our memories are (re)created in the present, then they also have the potential to be generative of meaning in relation to our future. In the wider context of the history of the council estate, and of its dwindling meaning in a time of acute, market-skewered and ownership-driven housing shortages, my memories of my childhood home could be construed as mere nostalgia. If so, then I'm happy with that, and I will press on regardless because, as Paul Ricoeur rightly said somewhere in his own studies of time, memory and nostalgia, "Nostalgia is to the emotions what idealism is to the intellect".

Imagined, Observed, Remembered

Peter Blegvad

When Marshall McLuhan observed that "the medium is the message" he was talking about technological hardware, but could this also apply to messages passing between areas of neurological 'wetware'—the brain and mind?

Consciousness is the product of innumerable synaptic feedback loops in which the brain communicates with itself: the faculties of imagination, observation and memory, for instance, are in constant correspondence with one another. It is these exchanges that enable us to negotiate the narratives of identity and difference required to navigate the world. But while this happens within a single consciousness, I think of imagination, observation and memory as separate specialised media, each sending messages with a different neurochemical 'tag' to differentiate them. The practical advantages of being able to tell a real lion from an imagined or remembered one, for example, are obvious. In matters of perception, the medium definitely is the message. Survival may depend on it.

This identification system can break down, however. When what we observe is mistakenly tagged as a memory we experience *déja vu*. When what we imagine is tagged as a memory we experience false memory syndrome. When what we imagine or remember is tagged as observation we experience hallucination. Or maybe we're dreaming.

Art encourages consciousness to relax the apartheid it normally enforces between these three faculties. It allows us to imagine "what if?" scenarios and to treat the impossible as real. Ambiguity and confusion—anathema to workaday logics—become aesthetic qualities to savour. And art itself produces feedback loops and interference, between our own memories, observations and imaginings and those of others.

Imagined, Observed, Remembered is an encyclopedic project that uses illustration to investigate, alter and expand consciousness. A three-step procedure is employed to produce pictures of things seen thrice:

1. *Imagined*: as a passive receiver, wearing a blindfold (a ganzfeld mask) I record descriptions of what I see in my mind's eye (hypnagogic images, remembered and imagined). I then make sketches as guides for further drawings.
2. *Observed*: as an active observer, my task is to find in the physical world correlatives for each imagined image and to draw them from visual references or from life.
3. *Remembered*: finally, from my memory of what I've imagined and observed, I create a simplified sign or icon, a reductive synthesis of previous data.

I depict them isolated in uniform white roundels against a black field, like specimens seen through a lens.

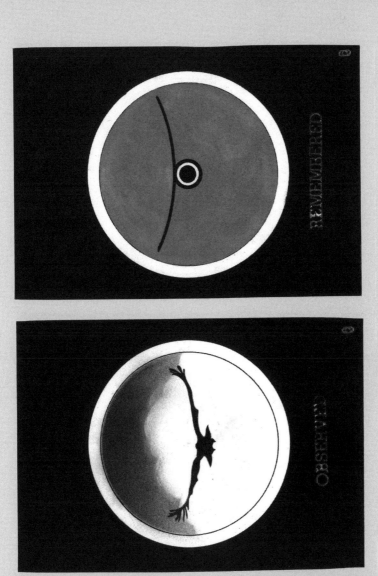

REMEMBERED

OBSERVED

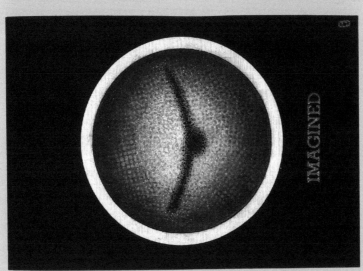

IMAGINED

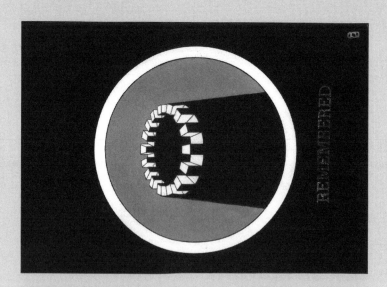

REMEMBERED

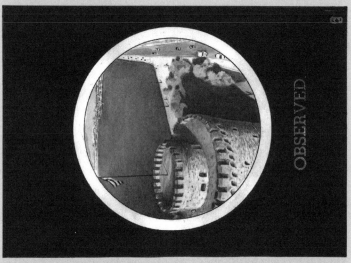

OBSERVED

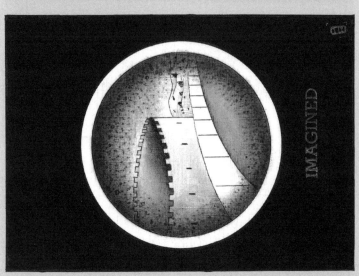

IMAGINED

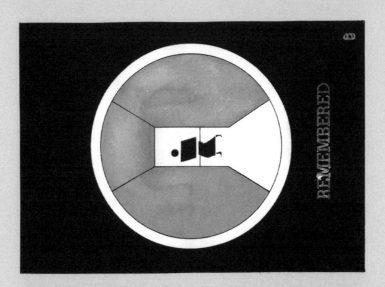

REMEMBERED

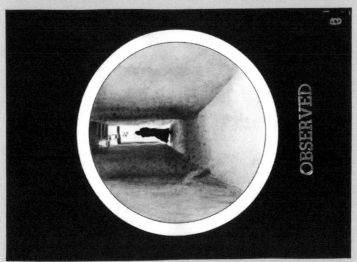

OBSERVED

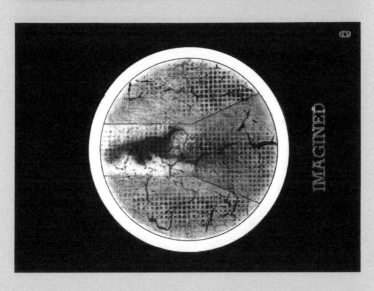

IMAGINED

REMEMBERED

OBSERVED

IMAGINED

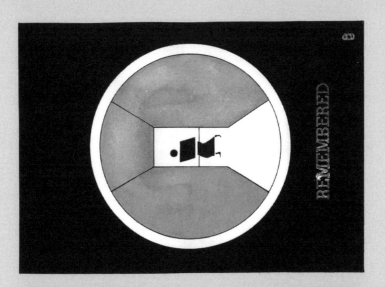

REMEMBERED

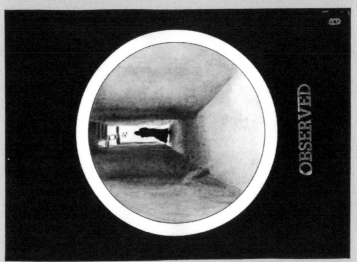

OBSERVED

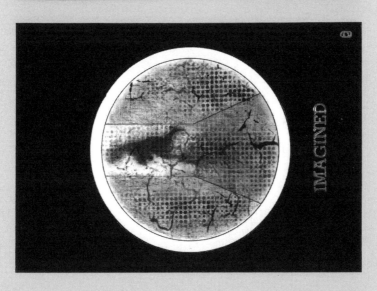

IMAGINED

REMEMBERED

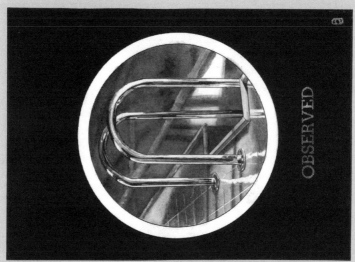

OBSERVED

IMAGINED

REMEMBERED

OBSERVED

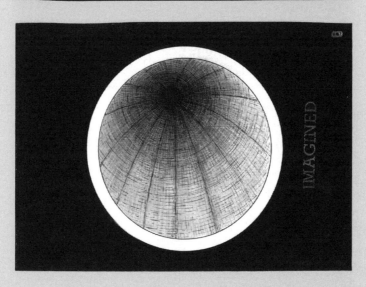

IMAGINED

A History of the Airfields of Lincolnshire

Simon Cutts

A History of the Airfields of Lincolnshire was first produced as a sewn section 32-page book in 1990. A frieze of poppies runs through the bottom of the pages, and the heads of their folds remained uncut, leaving them open at the bottom. Its cover was printed in green with its title in a darker green. The poem was also installed as a single wall in the Cairn Gallery in Gloucestershire in 1990, as a one-word poem, a title of any length and a single subject line. *A History of the Airfields of Lincolnshire II*, was then produced as a sewn section 32-page book by WAX366 in 2000, with a frieze of flax running at the top of the pages, and the tails of the folded pages remained uncut…

ppiespoppiespoppiespoppiespoppiespoppiespoppiespoppiespoppiespoppiesp

f   x f x f   x f x
x flax flax flaxflax flaxflax   flaxflax flax
axflax   flaxflax flaxflax   flaxflax flaxflax
x   f x f x   f x f

x f   x f x f
flax flax   flax flaxfla
flaxflax   flaxflax fl
f x   f x f x

34

                     x f   x f x f   x f x

flaxflax flax   flax flax flax flaxflax flaxflax   flaxflax flax
lax flaxflax   flaxflax   flaxflax flaxflax   flaxflax flaxflax
                     f x   f x f x   f x f

…leaving them open at the top. The cover was printed on linen covered blue board, with the title in dark green. In the intervening years since the first rendition of the poem, the predominant vegetation had changed from poppies to flax or linseed with its small blue flowers, the overspill of a change to a useable crop, and its name evocational of small bursts of explosion in the sky above, little clusters of anti-aircraft fire. In 2002 the poem was installed as anodised aluminium letters on slabs of excavated concrete runway placed at the side of the disused railway track outside Skellingthorpe, Lincolnshire, where it still remains. Grid Reference SK 934719.

Baswn i'n gweld y lle hwn, drwy eich gweledigaeth*

Phil Owen

I have slept the night many times on the side of this hill, through my life. Y Moelydd, the bald one. But I have never, for some reason, had any particular sense of its height, or shape. This strikes me as a difference in the way you approach a place as a child and an adult, the latter being more likely to subconsciously map it out, to maintain orientation.

I would have been happier to go on my own, but the old man came with me. Out of a sense of obligation, perhaps, or to see if he could still manage it. This old man, who has known me since before I was born, who I still refer to as my Uncle—though he isn't, and I am no longer a child—whose voice, thick with an accent you never, ever hear in the media, I have made recordings of. It was not warm and it was drizzling, but I wanted to go, and he seemed determined to come too.

We crossed the lane after a few dozen yards, by a house he pointed out as the one he used to live in. It is the site of one of my earliest memories—I'd accidentally broken a toy and put it back on a shelf, hoping nobody would notice—though I'd had no idea how close it was. We took a path, signposted as a stretch of Offa's Dyke, which runs along the side of the garden, and stopped, the first of many short rests, and wondered as to the new scaffolding on the house. The path as it led straight ahead was as steep as stairs, so he suggested an alternative, crossing over a field. I thought it best to take. He asked me if there was a stile in the hedge on the other side. I replied that there was, so we headed towards it.

Though we were only a hundred yards or so from his front door, he told me it had been years since he'd walked this way. The ground became more uneven as we went, and more overgrown. He slipped, quickly regaining his balance, but worrying me badly. If he fell and couldn't get up again, I would feel helpless, and embarrassed. I thought about insisting on taking him back and going on my own, but this would probably be taken as an insult. He climbed over the stile more easily than I expected. We came out on a lane wide enough for one car.

There was a house, looking out across a view that was already expansive. It was very quiet, but a man came out and went to his car. We exchanged pleasantries. His voice was northern English, and the house, a stone cottage, looked expensively kept. Passing this, and the driveway up to a farm, we went through a gate into a wood. It was dark with many yew trees, though they were young, and there was a flight of steps cut into the steep incline. We waited a while as he caught his breath, and he joked about his slowness. I wondered whether he could have a heart attack, what on earth would I do? I said something about the yew trees, though I was already tiring of conversation and struggling to sound interested.

The wood was small, and the steps didn't last long before we came out on open ground, divided by dry stone walls, several of them falling down. He asked me about

* 'Baswn i'n gweld y lle hwn, drwy eich gweledigaeth': I would see this place through your vision. The walk this piece of writing describes took place in the north-west corner of Shropshire, where some of my family come from. The area used to be widely Welsh-speaking, despite being east of the border. The legacy of the language continues there.

landmarks in front. There was a cottage. It was derelict, but there was still glass in the windows. It struck me as a perfect place to live.

By this point it was less clear where the top of the hill might be. I seemed to be navigating now, with his words of guidance, though I was unsure of whether we were following the route he was imagining. He told me, again, about how he used to come up here with the dog and the black haired young man, who I remember, who I suppose might have become his son-in-law. There was a strong smell of burning from the chimney of a farm just out of view.

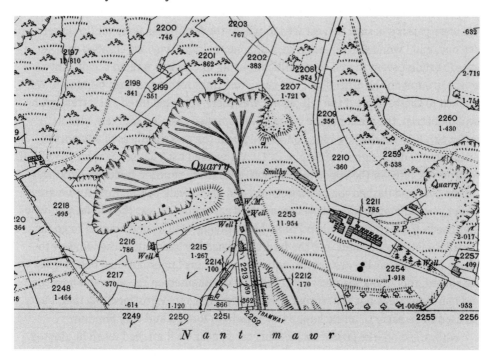

A slight elevation was suddenly obvious as the highest point in front of us, and I walked towards it, picking up pace, my attention to his need for care in navigating bumps and hollows in the ground (from old quarrying, he told me) being outweighed by my wanting to see the view from top. Like he'd said, at the highest point there was a sheet of metal etched with the compass points, and the directions and distances to other places. Both Yr Wyddfa and Cadair Idris were listed, about forty miles away each, and he told me that it would be possible to see ships on the Mersey. But the cloud was low, so I could only see the nearer hills, like clusters of rounded islands, and in the other direction the start of the flatter land. He called this the start of the Plains of Europe.

He suggested alternative routes to go back down. I chose the one that sounded the quickest and easiest. It would be less slippy underfoot, he said, but, as I soon realised, would not follow public footpaths. After walking a little way down the hill, a different direction from which we came, he asked me whether there was a gate in front of as. As we reached it, passing through a small herd of cows, a 'Keep

Out' sign on the gate came into focus. I had gotten cold, and the rain had become more insidious. I wondered whether we might get lost, whether the route followed by my being able to recognise the landmarks he could remember might disappear. We climbed over the 'Keep Out' sign, and he told me he knew the woman who had inherited the land from her father.

The small quarry looked fresh, the sides pale browns and orange. But there were no signs of activity, besides tire tracks churning the mud at our feet. Behind the hedges, I felt like I had lost my bearings and the opportunity of leading us back the way we had come. He told me about a hill farmer with a Welsh name whose land we were passing beside. He gestured to where the farmhouse was, but I couldn't see one, and I wondered whether we had gone the right way. We climbed another gate (he didn't seem to find these difficult, using his stick to fathom the distance to the ground on the other side), and came to a track leading to farm buildings. We walked to these, to see if the hill farmer was there. It looked utterly deserted, grim and industrial, the welcome the old man had implied seeming unlikely. I led us away, brightly persuading him, concerned about the awkwardness of any possible encounter and the signs warning of CCTV. We walked back along the track, downhill. A silver car came in the opposite direction, with a dog running beside it, barking. It pulled over and flashed the headlights. He told me to walk behind him. As we grew closer, the old man and the driver recognised each other. It was the hill farmer, who switched off his engine. "This is Philip, he is staying with us and wanted to go for a walk." I felt incongruous, but the farmer reached his hand out of the window to shake mine. (It was big and warm, with dirt under his fingernails like pencil lead). He smiled, though he seemed slightly shy. He commented on the wet, and how the old man's coat was not waterproof. I felt guilty, but as they gossiped together, I felt pleased to be party to an exchange that was both foreign and very familiar.

We walked on (the farmer had left his car in gear, so it lurched when he started the engine) and my sense of direction began to return to me. I recognised that we were approaching the road just outside the village, a bit further along from where we had started. He told me the farmer now lived in Oswestry, with his Mother. We passed old stone buildings that were once associated with the quarry. Some had been renovated. One was now a bunkhouse for walkers. I saw the white duvets of unmade beds through a window, but nobody appeared to be in.

We reached the road, and kept to the left, out of the way of the periodic cars. He complained how they drove too fast. One of the houses we passed was an older stone building, painted cream. I admired it, but he told me it had problems with damp, and was once occupied by a 'Bible basher'. We went back through the gate to the drive, and took our shoes off outside his house.

Mae gen i hiraeth ar gyfer y lle hwn, lle nad fi wedi byw, trwy etifeddiaeth, a trwy teimlo o bosibilrwydd. (I have a homesickness for this place, here where I have never lived, through inheritance and through a sense of possibility).

Near/Far

Rebecca Chesney

A tiny dot.
And another. And another.

Each an exit hole from a bark beetle on a tree trunk.
Years of drought have left Ponderosa, Jeffrey and Pinyon Pine trees most susceptible
to attack with the death toll an estimated sixty-six million in the Sierra Nevada.
The dead trees create a severe fire risk.

From a vast distance the planet is a patterned patchwork.
Blocks of dead trees killed by drought, bark beetle attack and fire are so huge they
can be plotted by satellite.

Every gesture we make and action we take has an impact.

A tiny dot is not insignificant.

Near: hand embroidery of bark beetle exit holes.
Far: print derived from NASA satellite imagery showing the extent of dead trees in Sierra Nevada.
For my dad: a truly wonderful and inspiring man 1 June 1938–3 November 2017.

Yorkshire Posts

Kevin Boniface

Sunday, 19 January 2014

A grey Vauxhall Zafira pulls up on the canal bank next to the narrowboat with the big spotlights—just down from where they pulled the dead paedophile out of the water in the Christmas holidays. A man gets out and sweeps half a dozen McDonalds take-out cups from the footwell and onto the towpath. He brushes crumbs from his fleece jacket and boot-cut jeans, stretches, gets back into the car and drives away.

The shadows of the people in the bus queue are long. The man I used to think looked too young to smoke a pipe is there, smoking a pipe. He doesn't look too young anymore. On the wall beside the shelter, someone has written 'I know' with a marker pen.

Hundreds of geese fly over in a noisy quarter-mile 'V' formation. The white UPVC front door of the house opposite opens—the one with the fake leaded lights in the shape of a Yorkshire rose—and Mr Mohammed steps outside in salwar kameez and sandals. He stands next to the soggy carpet in his front yard and looks up at the birds, shielding his eyes from the sun. Next door, the man in the torn gilet and jeans has also heard the noise and comes outside. He leans on his door frame holding a mug of tea in one hand, shielding his eyes with the other, his digestive biscuit held between his teeth. The two men stare up at the birds until they've all passed, briefly acknowledge one another and then go back inside, closing their front doors in unison.

Saturday, 1 February

As I pass the single, left-footed bowling shoe in the gutter—just before the pub chalkboard that's had 'Bitchcraft' written on it for weeks—a young man in a black tracksuit with white trim passes loudly, standing up on an exhausted old scooter. "That'll be stolen", says the toothless man with the tattoo teardrop from under his threadbare hoodie, "It's a wonder he's got a helmet on".

Mr Mahmood has paved over the paving that he paved over his garden with. He's laid some new, bright yellow concrete flags over the old cracked ones. He has used no bedding, mortar or fixture of any kind except at the edges where the flags adjoin his crumbling garden wall; just a lumpy smeared trail of cement runs around the perimeter joints.

Out in the sticks now, the wind is thrashing the trees and the sleet is thrashing my face as I slide around on slimy untreated millstone. It's been wet and windy for weeks and the verges are scarred with deep miry tyre tracks. Streams of run-off carry tree litter and even small branches along in the gutter. They are blasting at the quarry and a massive swirling flock of gulls is screeching overhead.

Two bald men in black tracksuits with white trim are overseeing the cross-country run around the perimeter of the school grounds. Dozens of teenagers straggle through the gap in the wall and splash past, all muddy ankles and too big t-shirts. A small, skinny boy with thick blond hair tells the taller heavier boy alongside him, "I was the fittest person with an inhaler at my old school".

In the valley bottom, where the moss on the dry stone walls is almost fluorescent, I watch a pair of herons flap by and disappear over the horizon where you can see the tips of the wind turbines on the moor.

At the cottage with the electric gates, a delivery driver rolls his eyes and says, "Twat", not quite under his breath as he tries to write out a form in a squall.

Tuesday, 18 February

The woman with the bit of cake on her face looks perplexed at the pair of boxing gloves in the road. It's raining hard, occasionally sleeting, and the deluged streets dance in reflected light. I cross to the street that's lined with empty pizza boxes, food tins, cooking sauce jars, energy drink cans, navy blue underpants, cerise pink shoes with missing heels, rolls of sodden carpet, mattresses, children's plastic ride-on toys, a sofa, broken glass, an empty satnav box, and a massive burst-open bag of aggregate. Near the top, at one of the houses where they have sold all the stone flags from the yard and replaced them with dog shit, the woman with the tattoos and the bathrobe says, "Ooo, it's snowing!" "I know", I say. "I take it you don't like snow." "No, not really, it's a bit inconvenient." "Haha! I do", she says, as she closes the door and disappears back inside her warm dry house. Next door, the stocky terrier on the windowsill is on its hind legs, pulling down the curtains, its cock flopping from side to side as it scrabbles its front paws against the glass, trying to get a better purchase.

It's still raining when I knock at the house with the crumbling concrete driveway to tell the owner of the S-Class Mercedes saloon with the low profile tyres that the driver's door is wide open. A man in his late-twenties answers. He wears a meticulously manicured beard, three-quarter length tracksuit pants, flip-flops and a T-shirt. "Yeah", he laughs, "I got to take it to the scrappers. Cheers, mate".

Sunday, 9 March

Two thin young men in snapbacks and bum fluff are eating eggs in the café on Westbourne Road, a copy of *The Sun* open on the table in front of them. "He paid £106,000 to look like that!" says the one in the white hat, poking his yolky knife at a picture of a semi-naked man with very pronounced abdominal muscles. "Why?" says the man in the blue hat. "Because he's a fucking knob."

At the Costcutter on the other side of the road, a young woman in a polka-dot onesie, heavy make-up, drawn on eyebrows and a big 'up do' is waiting outside in the drizzle with two Staffordshire bull terriers. A large truck passes, blowing over the steel Huddersfield Examiner sandwich board with a crash and the dogs yelp in surprise.

Later, out in the sticks, a pair of frogs are in amplexus on the steps of the house that once featured on TV's *Grand Designs* programme and a sparrowhawk kills a wood pigeon on Mr and Mrs Mitchell's driveway. As I cross the road by the Conservative Club, my hat blows off and a woman under an umbrella walks into me as I bend down to retrieve it.

On the estate, the man who always wears the same baggy tracksuit bottoms and unusual cap-sleeved t-shirt says he's looking forward to some nicer weather because it puts people in a better mood. Further down, in the car park by the flats, the old man in the tweed suit shouts "We're getting posh, aren't we?" to the Rastafarian man who is fitting some new wheel trims to his Vauxhall Astra.

Back in town, the drunk man in the grey suit is emptying his catheter bag into the storm drain by the bedroom furniture shop.

Tuesday, 1 April

The wind picks up and Mrs O'Leary's wind chimes chime while the scrap men throw the TV over the broken fence. Further down, the jolly old overweight racist man with the moustache and the 1970s zip-up raglan cardigan with suedette detail is hiding the Asian children's toys behind the wall at the bus stop again.

Down by the house with the ceramic cart horse in the porch, the kestrel perched on the steering wheel of the builder's van, stares as I pass. Next door, the woman who always calls me "My dear" is wearing her red coat with the leopard fur trim. She unloads Lidl and Wilko bags from a taxi, pays the driver and carries all six bags up her path at once, past the countless woodland creature garden ornaments that incorporate solar panels and lamps. I wave and she shouts "Hello, my dear!"

A funeral cortège led by a man in a top hat and a cane passes through the estate. Mrs Perkins adjusts her vest top and puts out her cigarette, "I don't know who that was", she says, "but you should always pay your respects, shouldn't you?"

At the large, detached houses near the park, an elderly man in a fleece jacket tells me, "Steam railways make life worth living".

At the house next-door-but-three—with the black BMW on the drive—another elderly man in a fleece jacket is in the garage. He's working at a Black & Decker Workmate while he listens to Ken Bruce play The Three Degrees on Radio 2. A Tesco delivery van arrives. The driver is also listening to Ken Bruce playing The Three Degrees on Radio 2, "How are you?" he shouts to the Black & Decker man. "I'd be a lot better if the sun was shining!" the Black & Decker man replies.

At the golf club, the four grey-haired golfers in black fleece jackets have gathered around the bearded, grey-haired golfer in the black fleece jacket to ask him how much they owe him. It transpires that three of them owe him £25.00 and one of them owes him £28.00.

Tuesday, 29 April

"I was out in fucking Leeds at the weekend", says the man sitting in front of me on the bus. "There's some fucking talent over there compared to Huddersfield, you know? It's a different world." "You need some bromide", says the man with the bent glasses next to him. "Bromide? What's bromide?" "It'll calm you down, stop you thinking about it all the time." "But I like thinking about it!" I look out of the window; a plump woman with thick dry curly hair is sitting at the lights in her mauve Vauxhall Corsa eating yoghurt from the pot with a metal spoon.

At the house with the single gatepost and a gate but no fence or wall etc., nothing to mark its boundary with the pavement, a boy of about ten years is standing and staring, his face smeared with streaks of fake tan. "How come you're just standing *there*?" he asks the delivery man, who's writing out a card on the step of the house next door. "How come you're just standing there?" the delivery man asks back. "I don't know", says the boy.

Out in the sticks, surrounded by dog groomers' vans, the sun comes out and flies bounce off my face. Trees cast dappled shadows across ivy-covered walls that buzz with insects. I hear a cuckoo, see dunlins, lapwings, pheasants, (close-up) swallows, ducks, geese, and a beautiful peacock butterfly, all within half an hour. Back in town, Craig Bainbridge tells me he's seen two ducks eating some chips outside C. Booth's hardware shop. He says he'd have taken a photo but he was on his scooter.

Touch

Les Coleman

Red felt-tip pen, toilet roll, 2006.

Google Landscapes

Tom Wilkinson

Having been through years of formal education in photography I have been conditioned to do things 'right', to forever be in search of the perfect picture. I was once described as a classical large format photographer and to an extent I agree. I shoot on film, take months and months to make new work, over-think everything and hide my light under the proverbial bushel. That's just me. So imagine my surprise when I discovered an instantaneous way of making photographs. Google Landscapes is that surprise.

It struck me one day, while researching new local cycling routes using Google Maps, that the visual and emotional reactions I get from some of the 'streetview' viewpoints very much align with my own feelings and opinions on landscape and the English countryside. Landscape as seen from the confines of a country road has a particular grammar, bearing both familiar and mundane qualities shared by those who travel through it. Blurred glimpses of fields through gateways, gaps in hedges and over brows of hills, perform like snapshots from a downbeat travelogue. This unique "blink or you'll miss it" way of experiencing the English landscape is frustrating in its urgency, often obscuring more than it reveals, but is likely one of the most commonly shared ways of viewing landscape.

As a nod to my large format sensibilities, I have cropped the screenshots I have appropriated from Google and converted them to black and white; a practically instant process compared to the lengthy, involved methodologies I use for other projects. The benefit of only using my smartphone means I am able to post the images on my Twitter account within minutes. It means that I can be current and spontaneous which I'm told is part of the point of social media, and as a publishing platform, why not? It seems fitting that the mode of the images' transmittal matches their mode of appropriation.

If I was to allow myself the indulgence and philosophise about this project, I would simply comment on the diverse range of photography consumption abundant today. The perfect picture, exquisitely printed, lauded by collectors and vigilantly archived for future generations has competition at last. Mass media and mass consumption, once thought of as a nuisance is, for me, now taking up an equivalent seat of power. What's the point of creating art if no-one is going to see it? Why not exploit the exploiter, play mass media at its own game, and use it as the pliable tool it has the potential to be?

My Google Landscapes are rogues with delusions of grandeur. Low-fi, low res, stolen images, dressing up in turn of the century garb. They don't know who or what they are meant to be and rely on their creators and viewers to give them a purpose.

Geeooggrraapphhy

Colin Sackett

Landscape is made of names and numbers as much as shapes and lines.—Anon.

It is obvious that in printing from a relief block those portions of the face of the block
which come in contact with the paper will produce corresponding solid marks on the
paper, whether they be lines, dots, or larger portions of the surface.
—Harry G. Aldis, *The Printed Book*. Cambridge, 1916.

Four maps from *London's Country, By Road, Stream and Fieldpath,*
Guide No.2, South of the Thames. London, c.1923: Abinger, Gomshall,
Wotton; Albury, Merrow Downs, Shere; Banstead Heath, Betchworth,
Reigate; Dorking, Leith Hill, Ranmore. Overprinted:

1. Abinger, Albury, Gomshall, Merrow Downs, Shere, Wotton.

2. Abinger, Banstead Heath, Betchworth, Gomshall, Reigate, Wotton.

3. Abinger, Dorking, Gomshall, Leith Hill, Ranmore, Wotton.

4. Albury, Banstead Heath, Betchworth, Merrow Downs, Reigate, Shere.

5. Albury, Dorking, Leith Hill, Merrow Downs, Ranmore, Shere.

6. Banstead Heath, Betchworth, Dorking, Leith Hill, Ranmore, Reigate.

7. Abinger, Albury, Banstead Heath, Betchworth, Dorking, Gomshall,
Leith Hill, Merrow Downs, Ranmore, Reigate, Shere, Wotton.

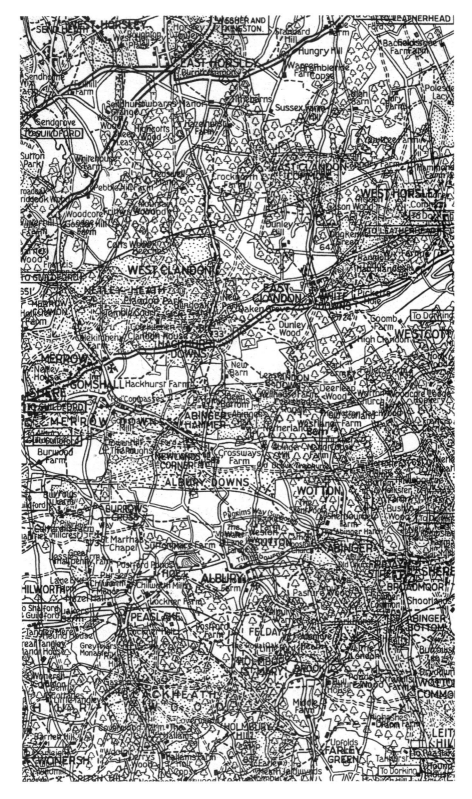

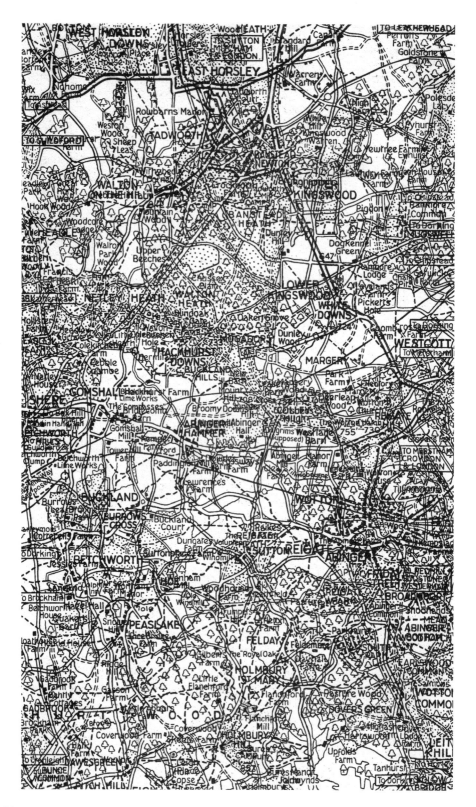

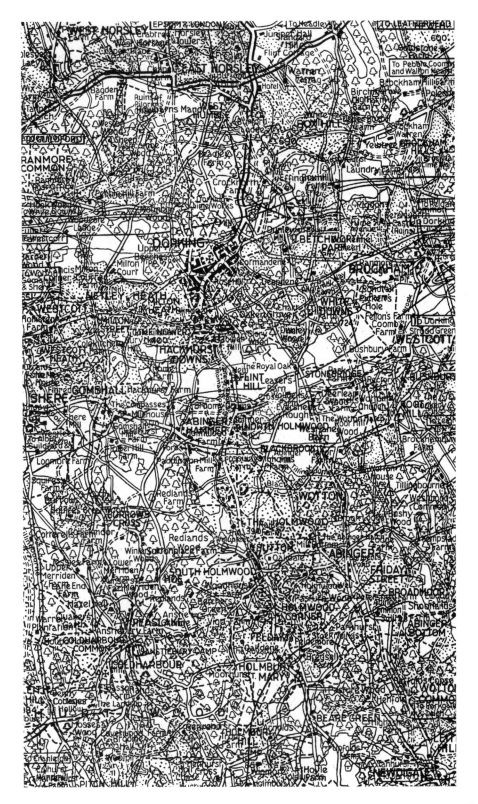

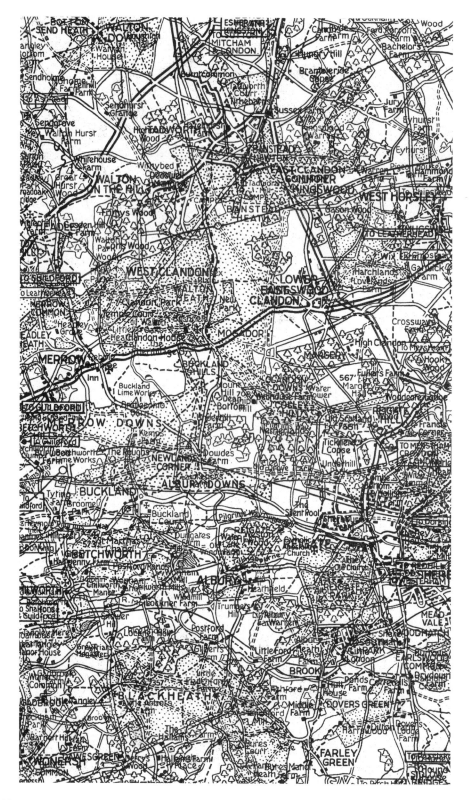

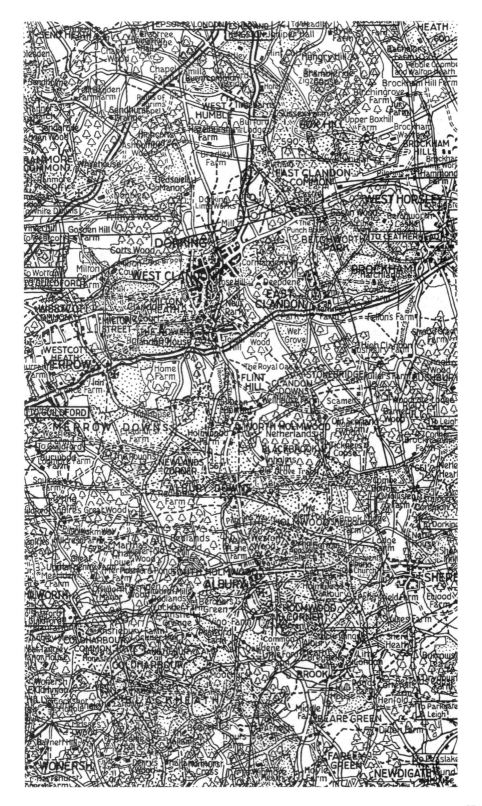

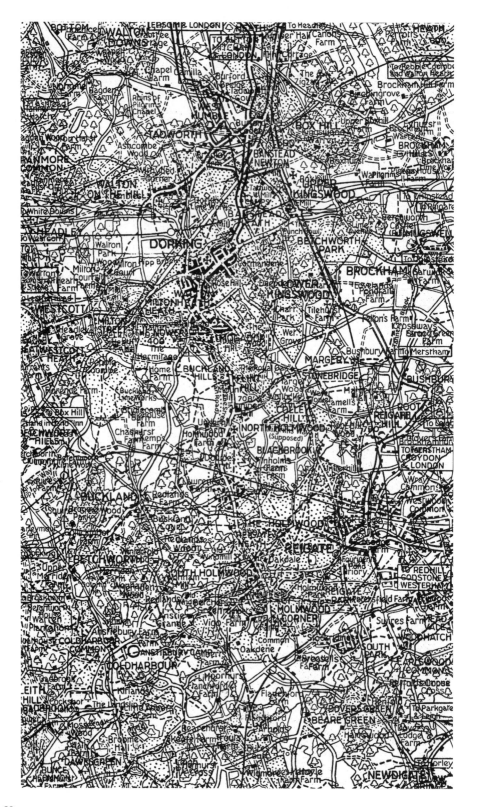

69

Barnetby–Grimsby

Brian Lewis

The wold cleansed, a whim
at every gate, effigies
lolling and pointing:
the road to Barnetby Top,
the blind cut to Gallows Wood.

Orbital junction,
an elevated section,
all lanes linked but one:
orphaned, unnamed, lulled, the home
of rabbits, foxes, field mice.

Elsham, the colours
are put away for the night,
each one in its fold.
The land is left to its shapes
and blue is the last to go.

The smuts are tethered
overhead, black laterals,
scudding into dross.
All the blotting parallels
backlit in a shelving mass.

Out in Beaumontcote
and the clutch of Beacon Hill
machines rasp and scour.
Overnight, the sheaves unclasp,
the tenderness inches back.

Softening shoulders,
a light in the town: slow signs,
a trough of flowers.
Sodium yellow outshines
this decorated border.

Years of truancy
abandon you to Queen Street's
Salvation Army.
Next door, a school museum,
the teachings of Wilderspin.

End of a branch line,
the nitrates unravelling,
one track, one buffer.
Beneath the platform, Barton
Haven, the heavy water.

Ropewalk, Waters' Edge,
the artificial harbour's
viewing area.
Canting to the cabled bridge,
arabesques of cowls and vents.

Midnight, the south shore
unsupervised, the clay pits
and wetland unclothed.
Underfoot, in brick paving:
eight points of a compass rose.

To each a new east,
a figment in the distance,
layer by layer,
the land remediated,
the way unaccompanied.

Reed beds, rinsed topsoil,
and before this, the tile works,
the mere, its white sails.
At the creek, a cement track,
black caustics, residuals.

Inshore, to Barrow,
then back through Old Ferry Wharf's
timber terminal.
How light and rhythm carry
from the scrapyards of Hessle.

Windmill Pond, a crux
with a scuffed nought, and always
the pontoon ahead.
Night thoughts, without complexion,
a path exhausting its chalk.

Port, line and station,
a pier and its passengers,
the old New Holland.
A cough, a yard half-open,
the tollman in his cabin.

The air blanketing,
dry bulk in weathered boxes,
unbreathing, behind
every shipment a tariff,
the covers laid for comfort.

3 a.m., Goxhill
approaching, a farmhouse caught
between embankment
and estuary, roof and glass
swept out, the gables aground.

Tin heaps at Neatgangs
sluice, the culvert frittering,
solids glancing off.
By the neap mark, a black dog,
shadowless, silent, single.

Cloud-chaff is total,
the Humber particulate,
the backlight snuffed out.
Pearling east, a white ship floats
one inch above the water.

Cyanotypes, strewn
over East Halton Skitter,
the flight calls of shanks
and sandpipers. The flood wall
sinking in the littoral.

Unregistered cars
in one zone, unregistered
vans in another,
the cargo of Killingholme,
counted out and counted in.

No path, only voids
between handling areas,
intermodal bays,
fenced compounds, serving notice
of extinguishment orders.

Dismantled railway,
the track bed now the field edge,
the cutting still mapped,
the line curving to South End
and no way of catching up.

Two years of night raids,
an airbase spent, a squadron
disbanded. Depots
where the Lancasters squatted.
Short-term, strategic, bonded.

St Margaret's, Habrough.
An old man at a headstone,
kneeling, renewing
a dry wreath, leaves for water,
returning to remember.

New links. Reburied
beneath the gyratory,
third party pipelines,
their high pressure diverted
from this bisected village.

A relief road, named
for a late lance corporal,
serving a remnant
of the Kingdom of Lindsey,
its low ceremonials.

At the roundabout,
four exits, the greens maintained,
the apron uncreased.
This turn for the Oldfleet Drain
and Healing to the near east.

Ciba, Tioxide.
The ancient rights of Great Coates:
warren and wreckage,
its armed manorial moat
a grant of the exchequer.

A continent's aid
at crofts' end: all trades converge
on Europarc, raise
Innovation, Pegasus,
Origin and Genesis.

Barnetby to Grimsby (via Barton and the Humber), 13–14 August 2016.

Hull–Spurn Point

Brian Lewis

At the muster point,
a memory's corrections,
errors in the path.

Ocean Boulevard,
the ornamental water
on the patent slip.

Technology park,
logistics park, prison, port
and chemical park.

The quayside falling
behind dredging and infill,
trailers hauled inland.

Bridging the old fleet,
the new freight. Minerals fuse,
heat cogenerates.

One note from the plant,
another from the waste tank:
descant without end.

Holmen Carrier,
intertidal, small and blue,
to the night alone.

Leaving Paull Holme Strays,
half the reedbed realigned,
its songs caught and lost.

Only the salt marsh
and a dormitory adrift,
quartering the dark.

Drain and counter drain,
a path without companion,
half and half again.

Midnight, incoming.
A radar mast, buffering
the sandbars and buoys.

Stone Creek, bone-dry yachts,
the byway now a boatyard,
an isle off the chart.

Immingham, the flare
and fastness, outfall and steam,
glitzing to stacked glare.

White point, softening,
the air sticks to everything,
withdrawal and sweats.

Zero longitude.
The moon yellows, slips into
a pocket of cloud.

A spike in the sluice.
The stations of Outstray Lane,
the light at my back.

Lapse of permission:
dissolving the Wapentake's
unmanned garrisons.

Soak Dike, little tern
plumbing the salt pools, skimming
the fissuring clays.

The body, the hours
running down at the mudflats,
too late for repair.

The ends of tillage,
ends of leisure, the bygones
on a tilting shelf.

At the Humber mouth,
a demilitarised spit
and its tumbled squibs.

Scruff of the cuspate,
wisps of fibre: a scarf snagged
on this neck of land.

The road falls to bits.
An island in the making
and the line extinct.

South of the Narrows,
beached in concrete and marram,
an unlatched shelter.

This sliver of rail,
a storm-shuffled arrowshaft
breaking in mid-flight.

Saving the lighthouse.
The last families on Spurn,
leaving the lifeboats.

Neither heel nor head,
but a thin, hooked tail, turning
landward and seaward.

Hull to Spurn Point, 16–17 July 2016.

Modernist Dartmoor

Matthew Kelly

"A 750-ft mast on this height would dominate the surrounding country with inescapable ubiquity. Its alien presence and associations would be a perpetual reminder of that modern 'civilisation' which most people come to a national park to forget. The tor itself would disappear. Twenty-five acres of its summit would be 'acquired' for the spread of the mast's steel supports, and the buildings, of the well-known BBC-type—flat-topped rectangles like petrified railway carriages—would crown the tor in place of its natural rocks, for they are normally sited close to the mast. Undoubtedly a road and a concrete platform, fencing, pipes, electricity and telephone cables would also accompany the mast to the summit of the tor. It would be landscape-slaughter on a more than usually impressive scale."
—Dartmoor Preservation Society, 10 December 1951

"We cannot agree that a graceful engineering structure such as a Television mast would destroy for ever the wild and natural character of a very wide area of ancient hill-country landscape, particularly as we want to erect it fairly close to Dartmoor Prison which is by no means a place of beauty."
—Edward Bonong, BBC engineer, 6 February 1952

I know I'm wrong, but I still think it white. A wand,
a conductor's baton; pristine, Kittiwake elegant,
the technological sublime. Concorde? Yes, that's it.
Concorde possessed my childhood imagination and
this lancing form seemed of its essence.

I was twenty years out. It's not of Concorde,
the Intercity, the Thames Barrier, the triumphant
death rattles of the dirigiste state. It's early '50s
monochrome, before the white heat. Gave telly,
though, to cold British rooms.

And it is not an aerial. Got that wrong too. A
frame, that's all, latticed and functional. A mast.
Things hang from masts. Flags and sails. This mast
is barnacled, raised maculate from the deep. Now
largely redundant but now wanted. Makes the moor
navigable, they say.

I thought it stood unaided, stabbed into place,
vibrating with that founding energy, a tuning fork
on a baby grand. Thick steel cabling guy it, pinioned
tight, must always face the wind. The sky from the
base is scored with dark lines.

What is Dartmoor and what is it for? The mast
reframed the question, as now it partitions the sky.
Extending into view on the eastern approach to
the Warren Inn, there on the western horizon at
Buckland Beacon, those four red lights in the night.
Does it gauge Dartmoor, making it small?

Beneath is prison, old quarries and spoil,
brewery, railway scar. Granite stumps record
prisoners that died. Just initials and a date. Fresh
white houses, too. Embourgeoisement? Hardly.
A whiskey distillery is coming. Duchy land this,
no freehold. Princetown, the prince's town.

Black and white photos fake a '50s aesthetic.
Official publications, *Architectural Review*. A clean,
austere beauty giving scale to the sky. Except the
buildings are granite. A hokey concession. Practical
Rustic. A style undeserving a theorist.

They saved the gale-layered granite of North
Hessary, de-naturalising the rock. Trig point made
it too, collaterally. The cabling was buried. This
assemblage is now preserved, its obsolescence given
sanctuary, a reliquary of a past iteration of the state.

Braque's Postcards

Janet Boulton

Our week-long visit in early September to Varengeville-sur-Mer was in the nature of a pilgrimage to where Georges Braque had spent much of his working life since 1928. Perhaps to catch a glimpse of his house and studios in the Chemin Braque, visit the Eglise St Valery and his grave in the cemetery on the clifftop, and to walk down the long Descente du Petite Ailly leading to the famous beach. Braque made about forty paintings of this part of the north Normandy coast—the sea, the cliffs, the beach with its wrecks and rocks. He called these small works, scarcely ever more than sixty-five centimetres in width, "my little postcards".

With the idea to make some pictures of the place where he liked to walk every day, and knowing how central the materials of his trade were to Braque's way of thinking about painting—he served an apprenticeship as a painter and decorator—I chose to take four small sheets of heavyweight watercolour paper, two soft carpenter's pencils, two flat sable brushes and eight colours. Remembering his *Pensées et réflexions sur la peinture* from 1917—"the goal is not to be concerned with reconstituting an anecdotal fact, but with constituting a pictorial fact" or as I once read "nothing must stand in the way of making a picture a true pictorial fact", I wasn't especially concerned to establish exact locations for his beach paintings.

The time spent on the beach was greatly enhanced by the weather. Dark skies, squalls of rain, high wind, and turbulent waves, the expanses of sand with fluorescent-yellow-green pools, strange rocks smooth and pock-marked, chunks of white chalk amongst flint pebbles. All this contained within the long shallow curve of the cliffs, stretching from the west end of Varengeville to Pourville and Dieppe five miles away to the east. Braque wasn't a painter of good weather.

We picked up odd bits of gossip—that the studio in Chemin Braque was much as he left it—his hundreds of brushes still in their pots, his palettes hanging on stands fabricated from driftwood; and that the garden was about two hectares and contained two ponds. Our attempt at trespass was foiled by the rusting hinges of the dark green gates and a dense overgrowth of laurel and bamboo. The place had been shut up since his wife Marcelle's death in 1965, while the inheritor of the property, her nephew, remains unresponsive to any local concern about his legacy.

According to Alex Danchev, writing in his *Georges Braque: A Life*, published 2005, Varengeville is little visited specifically for Braque. This network of winding roads and leafy lanes shaded by splendid beech trees planted on high banks and discrete villas behind well-trimmed hedges, would be a very different place if a museum were to come into being. Would Braque have minded its absence—he initiated nothing in his lifetime and apparently left no official instructions as to the future of the house. It is said that Braque is a painter's painter and it seems it is poets and other artists that continue to be his most enduring testament.

Walks from City Bus Routes

J. R. Carpenter

During the summer of 2009 I spent a week reading and writing in residence at the Elizabeth Bishop House, in the tiny and thus somewhat incongruously named village of Great Village, Nova Scotia. Readers may know Great Village as the setting of Bishop's haunting story 'In the Village', first published in *The New Yorker* in 1953. One day I went for a walk to the village store. I was on the hunt for postcards, intrigued by Bishop's observation: "The grey postcards of the village for sale in the village store are so unilluminating... one steps outside and immediately sees the same thing: the village, where we live, full-size, and in colour".

In the back of the store, which is now an antique shop, I happened upon a well-preserved copy of a *City of Edinburgh Transport Map* published by the Edinburgh Geographical Institute in the 1940s. Nova Scotia being New Scotland, an old map of Old Scotland seemed a perfectly reasonable thing to find. Why I felt the need to buy an out-of-date-map to a city I'd never been to was somewhat less clear.

Questions of place and displacement have long-pervaded my fiction writing and maps have figured prominently in many of my web-based works. An outline of a map of Nova Scotia served as the interface for one of my earliest web-based works, *Mythologies of Landforms and Little Girls* (1996). In *The Cape* (2005), I used an assortment of maps, charts, and diagrams borrowed from an *Environmental Geologic Guide to Cape Cod National Seashore* published in 1979 as stand-ins for family photographs. In *In Absentia* (2008) I used the Google Maps API to haunt the satellite view of the Mile End neighbourhood of Montreal with stories of former tenants forced out by gentrification. My first novel, *Words the Dog Knows* (2008) included an impossible map of ancient Rome. I'd never set out to map a place I'd never been before, but then sometimes maps seem to call places into being.

In 2011 I was commissioned to create a new work for an exhibition called 'Remediating the Social', at Inspace gallery in Edinburgh. Handily I already had a map of the city. In May 2012 I travelled to Edinburgh to begin research for what would eventually become a massive hybrid print and digital project called *The Broadside of a Yarn* (2012). More information on that project can be found in an article called 'The Print Map as a "literary platform"' published on *The Literary Platform* in May 2013.

During my research I used the 1940s edition of the *City of Edinburgh Transport Map* purchased in Great Village, Nova Scotia, to undertake a series of experimental walks, or *dérives*, in and around the modern city of Edinburgh. In his *Formulary for a New Urbanism* (published under the pseudonym Gilles Ivan) Ivan Chtcheglov proposes a future city, in which "the main activity of the inhabitants will be CONTINUOUS DRIFTING" (1953). In *The Beach Beneath the Street: The Everyday Life and Glorious Times of the Situationist International* (2011), McKenzie Wark suggests that Chtcheglov "sought not the rational city but the playful city, not the city of work but the city

CITY OF EDINBURGH
TRANSPORT MAP

Transport Offices :
2 St James Square

ROBERT M'LEOD, M.Inst.T.
Transport Manager

Telephone Nos. 24071-5

of adventure. Not the city that conquers nature, but the city that opens toward the flux of the universe". The advertising copy on the back of the *City of Edinburgh Transport Map* hovers between these states—on one hand promoting such solid stolid institutions as the Bank of Scotland, North British Rubber Footwear, and Scougal's Oatcakes, "Scotland's National Food in its Most Palatable and Convenient Form"—and on the other hand issuing imperatives toward the exploration of a playful city, a city of adventure, and, read from a contemporary vantage point, a city safely adrift in simpler past:

> *Follow the Star of Health.*
> *Encompass the City.*
> *Map it Out For Yourself.*
> *Do Not Allow Your Holiday to be Spoiled by Rain.*

However many times I set out toward the flux of the universe in search of the points of interest advertised on the map—"The Largest Stock of Hand-Knitted Woollies in Britain", "Radiator and Mudwing Repairs and Other Sheet Metal Work", "Vertical Filing Systems and Visible Card Index", and "Carpenter Joiner Jobbing Specialists", orders in any part of the city or elsewhere in towns or country promptly attended to—*dérive* led me instead into Edinburgh's wealth of museums, libraries, and used and antiquarian print, map, and book shops.

In the Old Town Bookshop I found an A5-sized staple-bound booklet called *Walks from City Bus Routes* published by Edinburgh City Transport in the late 1950s. This booklet contains twenty-two narrative descriptions of walks, each beginning and ending within easy reach of bus routes, and each illustrated by a small black and white line drawing. The preface states: "this book is designed for the visitor or the resident who wishes to have a change from the more usual places of tourist interest and to combine a little mild exercise with exploration of the lesser known parts of the city and suburbs". The unnamed author adds that her one wish "is that those who follow these trails derive as much pleasure from them as she has done over the years".

Many of the lesser known parts of the city and suburbs the author urges us to explore are no longer know-able. Many of the green spaces on the *City of Edinburgh Transport Map* have long since filled in. Time has rendered these two immutable print documents nearly nonsensical. I decided to further this process.

I created a computer-generated narrative called *Walks from City Bus Routes* which uses JavaScript to randomly and endlessly recombine illustrations and portions of text from the Edinburgh City Transport booklet and bus and tram route icons from the *City of Edinburgh Transport Map*. The term 'computer-generated' is something of a misnomer here. The computer does not generate these new texts. It selects phrases from the booklet which I have typed into preset lists (variable strings) and slots them into templates (sentences). Take, for example, the following sentence:

Take the #{take} and continue #{continue}.

I went through the print booklet looking for phrases which follow the words "take" and "continue". Let's say the phrases which follow #{take} are as follows (there are in fact many more than these):

> Take the ['path leading down the hillside just before the monument', 'path that leads off to the left', 'broad and easy descent down the grassy slope', 'towpath along the side of the park', 'dirt road that runs uphill under the wall', 'road behind the Inn']

And the phrases which follow #{continue} are:

> continue ['upstream', 'to follow the river', 'in the same direction', 'through the fields', 'as far as the roundabout','along the High Street to the old parish church set in a green graveyard', 'in a roughly southerly direction', 'to follow the wall']

Here are but a few of the possible sentence results:

> Take the path leading down the hillside just before the monument and continue along the High Street to the old parish church set in a green graveyard.

> Take the towpath along the side of the park and continue in the same direction.

> Take the broad and easy descent down the grassy slope and continue through the fields.

Though many of the paths, towpaths, grassy slopes, fields, and roundabouts referenced in the Edinburgh City Transport pamphlet no longer exist, as variables within JavaScript strings these past places are ascribed new locations in computer memory. Called as statements into this new narrative structure, these past places become potential (albeit imaginary) destinations once again (albeit for readers rather than walkers).

The result is a new guide 'book' which perpetually proposes an infinite number of plausible yet practically impossible walking routes through the city of Edinburgh, and its bookshops, confusing and confounding boundaries between physical and digital, reading and walking, fact and fiction.

In the gallery installation of *The Broadside of a Yarn* exhibited in Edinburgh during 'Remediating the Social' in November 2012, this new digital variable iteration of the *Walks from City Bus Routes* pamphlet was accessed by scanning a QR code embedded in a cartographic collage which remediated elements of the *City of Edinburgh Transport Map* and a drawing borrowed from the *Edinburgh Streetscape Manual*, published by the Lothian Regional Council in 1995. These visual links to the work were also reproduced in an A3-sized print map iteration of *The Broadside of a Yarn*, which was handed out freely during the exhibition and continues to circulate through gift exchange economies and postal networks. A stand-alone web-based version of *Walks from City Bus Routes* was published in the Spring 2015 issue of *The New River: a journal of digital writing & art*.

Walk more quickly.
Walk more slowly.
Take another walk.
Stop walking.
Walks ABOUT.

WALKS FROM CITY BUS ROUTES

DIRECTIONS: Leave the bus and turn left to the first opening past the public park. Take the nearest path, which crosses the grass diagonally and continue in a roughly southerly direction. Note that on the map, proposed tramway extensions are shown thus: ████████ Passing disused quarry you will note an old stone bridge. Here there are many attractive streets. The fine outlook over the weir can present quite an awesome spectacle in times of spate, with the brown water racing over the apron in a smooth silent curve. The convent, now a college, was a hospital for shell-shocked and psychiatric cases in the first World War. Turn Right along the first opening beyond the canal and follow the road to the top of the hill. Seats, strategically placed here, give a good excuse for a rest. On a hot day in summer a stroll along the promenade may be a little tiresome. From this point, cross the hotel car park. Continue in the same direction. This walk is at its best in early autumn or late spring. The rather scrambly path along the edge of the trees is death to weak ankles. The drive leads to the bus route at the bridge. Note that on the map, tram and bus services are shown at the termini thus: ⑥ 🄗 For bus route information see appendix.

Walk more quickly.
Walk more slowly.
Take another walk.
Stop walking.
Walks ABOUT.

WALKS FROM CITY BUS ROUTES

DIRECTIONS: Leave the bus and walk west to the first opening on the right. Take the second path from the north and continue along the bus route between private houses on the left and army property one the right. Note that on the map, proposed tramway extensions are shown thus: ████████ Passing a bowling green you will observe a gate. Here there is a kiosk for refreshments. Here the stream flows under the embankment of the road. This is a very ancient open space. Turn Left across the bridge and follow the Queen's drive westward. Through the window-embrasures there is a fine view of the weir. The Rose Garden and the Italian Garden are particularly attractive in summer. On reaching the road, cross the old bridge. Continue straight ahead along the private avenue to the hospital. This walk is not advisable after a spell of wet weather. Watch out for red flags. The road continues between the grounds of the hospitals to the bus route. Note that on the map, tram and bus services are shown at intervals along the routes thus: ④ 🄔 For bus route information see appendix.

```
Walk more quickly.
Walk more slowly.
Take another walk.
Stop walking.
Walks ABOUT.
```

WALKS FROM CITY BUS ROUTES

DIRECTIONS: Leave the bus and enter the garden by the east gate. Take the path that leads off to the left and continue as far as the roundabout. Note that on the map, proposed tramway extensions are shown thus: ▓▓▓▓▓▓▓ Passing the main entrance to the quadrangle you will come to a road close to the shore. Here there are kingfishers nested in the quiet shrubberies of the cemetery walls. The first touch of frost produces a vivid tawny orange in the leaves. Here, in 1513, the original wall led off behind the present school. Turn Left at the Hotel and follow the eastmost wall to the commercial centre of the port. The view over these fields is superb on a clear day. The best time of year is early June, when lilac and laburnum in profusion overhang old stone walls and the great trees are still in fresh green. A few yards along, cross the street and walk to the right until you come to three paths crossing the meadows. Continue as far as the roundabout. This walk follows the farming fringe of the city. The first section of this path is rough and unpleasant, but it soon opens out. In the summer busses are extended. Note that on the map, tram and bus services are shown at the termini thus: ⊜ ⊞ For bus route information see appendix.

```
Walk more quickly.
Walk more slowly.
Take another walk.
Stop walking.
Walks ABOUT.
```

WALKS FROM CITY BUS ROUTES

DIRECTIONS: Leave the bus and strike uphill. Take the path and continue right down the road and turn right. Note that on the map, motor bus routes are shown thus: ▓▓▓▓▓▓▓ Passing around the scenic side of the pond you will reach an almost exclusively academic thoroughfare. Here there breweries, owing to the properties of the water peculiar to the natural springs. The fenced-in portion of rock was scored by glaciers at the end of the ice age. The convent, now a college, was a hospital for shell-shocked and psychiatric cases in the first World War. Turn Right at the Road and follow the track that leads under the arches of the new bridge. The view of the city from this point is among the finest in the area. The last section is the most attractive in early autumn when the sun is setting behind the dark woods. A short distance to the right, cross the street. Continue on the path which follows the edge of the hill to emerge beside the school. This walk requires a minimum of exertion. A path constructed on the often precipitous banks right along the river. You will find a footbridge and a seep path leading up to the road less than half a mile west of the bus terminus. Note that on the map, tram and bus services are shown at intervals along the routes thus: ⓪ ⊞ For bus route information see appendix.

Mud

Caitlin DeSilvey

A digger's beep and grind casts a strangely urban acoustic up the hill over the calm lawns of the big house. I follow the noise. Down in the valley the men and their machines are improving the lake. I sit on a stone bench to watch. Improvement is a messy business. The toothy bucket of the yellow JCB scrapes a mouthful of dark muck from the lake edge and slops it into the hopper of a giant mechanical wheelbarrow.

I can't see where they are putting the mud, but I can see where they put it this morning. A foot thick layer of lake muck spills down the slope behind me. The manufactured mudslide flows around the trunks of young oaks and spattered the glossy leaves of a rhododendron thicket. It has now firmly set and its surface is dusted with a russet scatter of sycamore leaves. The flow stops an arms length from the infant river Lerryn.

I follow the river's course in my mind, under the steep banks of autumn oak, over the beds of the caddis flies and the salmon fry, around the stepping stones in Lerryn village and out to where it joins the Fowey, just above the mussel beds, before the river turns at the china clay docks. I think about what will happen in the next rainstorm. I think about all that mud.

I dodge the wheelbarrows to climb the far hill, past a field slope where the muck lies thick over fruiting brambles and flattened bracken. Pheasants spook as I skirt the edge of the wood. A few hundred yards along I come across another earthwork. A large chunk of the hillside has been scooped away to leave deep gouge in the raw reddish soil. The space levels down to a flat platform with a fine view back to the house. The indentation in the earth is as even and unsettling as the thumbprint I found pressed into the cream on top of my cake at lunch.

Les Coleman *Mud*, photograph (detail), 1977.

Styan

Nathan Walker

Styan: West Cumbrian for 'stone'.

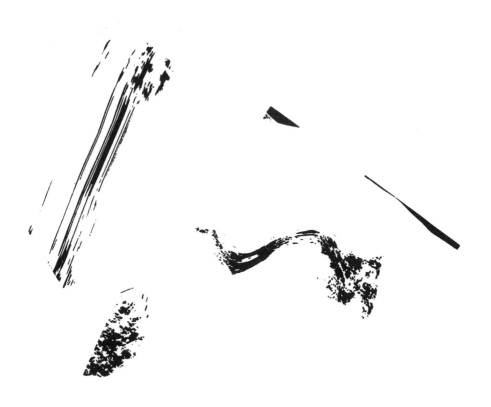

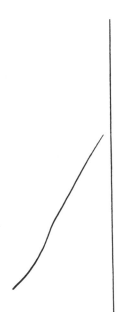

The Downs

Angus Carlyle

9:41am, Jun 21 2016: Early grey skies open to blue, cold to heat, scent of seeding grasses, rabbits over clearings and under hedges, birdsong still turned to 11. / 6:04pm, Jul 1 2016: Top of the Downs, wind shells my ears from every point of the compass, skylark song chopped, two wood pigeons startled into staying still. / 11:22pm, Jul 3 2016: An interval hour: from dew on the plastic chair and The Plough bright against the dark sky to mottled cloud spreading across the quiet. / 11:21am, Jul 13 2016: Paths in the woods remember last night's rain, paths by the roads have forgotten, paths of the hills do some of both. / 5:20pm, Jul 18 2016: Crickets pulsed electric, barley on last turn towards gold, wind made shimmer a verb of sound, paragliders launched off the iron age fort / 9:31am, Jul 24 2016: Purple pelt of clouds, orange moon a pale river bulb, silver creeks point home, insects swarm in torch cones, moths' soft short stays, joy. / 9:33am, Jul 24 2016: Hobbled over the line in a daze, toenails hurt, toes hurt, heels hurt, shins hurt, calfs hurt, thighs hurt, arse hurts, knees agony, happy / 1:56pm, Jul 29 2016: Chalkdust on our shoes, hot under the grey and the wind, butterflies fold and unfold where they find shelter. / 10:18am, Jul 31 2016: Avian song duel in turns: jackdaws stalk chimneypots tutting; young gulls wheeze in hunger, adults stretch out ornate gurgles and screams. / 12:03am, Aug 14 2016: Look up from smells of stripped lavender heads on my finger-tips to see a shy-bold fox cub on a wall, watching me. / 6:08pm, Aug 18 2016: Out in the open, squinting in the air that still simmered; cooler under the trees, the path dappled, bright diagonals on trunks and leaves. / 3:51pm, Aug 20 2016: On the ridges, rain sheets cold around the compass rose, puddles rising rapidly on summer-dried paths; in the woods, canopies wind-shrieked. / 5:03am, Aug 22 2016: Sliced chalk moon, mist curls through the valley, swifts twist screeching beneath the arch, the cries then bounced around the architecture / 11:22pm, Sep 8 2016: Late night street run: torn clouds, stars dot between, wind ruffles then fritters, no birdsong but distant siren, voices raised in laughter / 11:14pm, Sep 9 2016: Salt-skin run: the city to the Dyke, over Truleigh Hill, hot to the river then home, past a clacking pylon with postcard sky views. / 1:56pm, Sep 11 2016: Special day on the Downs: crow shadow on corn stubble; thousands of seed clocks drift, glint; buzzards mew; the far blurred, the near sharp / 9:08pm, Sep 28 2016: In the nimbus of tonight's head torch: beaded threads of rain, sprays of saliva, billows of breath, my hand bringing the bottle to my mouth. / 5:00pm, Sep 30 2016: New shoe conkers; bursts of scarlet berries; rain-laden cloud that didn't empty; and the last 5 miles: running as puppetry (with added bile) / 6:32pm, Oct 7 2016: On the last stretch, shafts of light dropped from clouds onto the skylines, where the shafts fell to the sea they spotted pools of silver. / 5:09pm, Oct 9 2016: Slow turn of the woods gives smells of: wet dog, faint soap on hand, bonfire smoke, horse dung, perfume, 2-stroke exhaust, musty dry leaves. / 7:03pm, Oct 14

2016: Not quite rain, more the air perspiring; winds soft in the hollows and fiercer on the ridges, bringing the season's cold with an early dark. / 12:21pm, Oct 23 2016: Morning wind rushing trees, whispering dry reeds and crackling oak, willow and sycamore leaves down the river paths. No kingfishers. / 5:33pm, Oct 23 2016: On twilit way out: Cold, goosebumps, rueing lack of clothes. On dark way back: Sweaty hot, stripping off jacket, peeling off gloves. / 7:11pm, Nov 5 2016: Fireworks arc into the concrete skate bowls, detonating in coloured flashes, sprays of sparks, booms and crackles, huge smoke clouds, oaths. / 6:23pm, Nov 7 2016: Orange stripes cast by trunks and 53 blue-black crows at first dewpond: sipping, striding, swaying on branches, soaring and sliding the sky / 6:29pm, Nov 7 2016: Litterfall as deep as I've ever seen it, obscuring paths and tree roots and flints; the leaves incredible colours in vivid to muted shades. / 2:43pm, Nov 14 2016: 16 skiving miles: partridge blurs,

flock calligraphics, wind gusts, rain plucking crops, puddles deepen, gorse flowered, heli over prison. / 6:47pm, Nov 18 2016: Beaters line with white flags, shots from behind sound in front; sun glows buzzard wings; shepherdess herds almost perfect circle of sheep. / 2:59pm, Nov 20 2016: Sulphide scents between each gust, skins salted by the air, the lights changing second by second, seabirds now white, now silver, now black. / 4:24pm, Nov 28 2016: Balsdean: walker had shadow, but not her dog; birds changed from white to black; crow flight ragged yet no wind; warm ridge, ice in the dip. / 4:41pm, Nov 28 2016: One last gift from the falling sun: Old Man's Beard set aglow like a lantern mantle. / 3:17pm, Dec 18 2016: Mists curl beneath Firle Beacon, gaps open then seal shut, Mt. Caburn disclosed then obscured. Jackdaws reveal their name as onomatopoeia. / 6:28pm, Dec 21 2016: Scurries in undergrowth, wing flaps from canopy, skating smooth mud and soaking through puddles, moths and spittle in torch halo: dark woods / 12:39pm, Jan 2 2017: Glittering waves sound out as they strike the pebbles under the sea wall to my right then are audible again on the left echoing off cliff. / 11:32am, Jan 30 2017: Waves crackle the pebbles, spray coats skin with salt, gulls and petrels wheel, dive and bob, phone shutters tick and flashes, sky lightens. / 12:39pm, Feb 2 2017: Rain drenched: "Violent Queer" graff, green back of startled yaffle, moss in the copse, furrows from stolen moped, slope circling dew pond. / 10:28pm, Feb 7 2017: Lovely moon halo. / 6:13pm, Feb 9 2017: From the First Dewpond through the woods, past the stadium and up to the phone mast then down the slope between the dank gorse to Ballsdene. / 5:48pm, Feb 11 2017: A wet snow clung to the Downs, weighing the gorse, pushing the far further, dusting oblivious sheep, softening the heard, making me gambol. / 9:07pm, Feb 17 2017: Something withheld, the land holding its breath then fog descends then the dark and I am completely lost, spooked by cows, snagged on fences / 9:30pm, Feb 17 2017: Sweet brock, white whole teeth, bright fur, no visible injuries but from position of its corpse on the verge, doubtless the result of a car. / 2:13pm, Feb 19 2017: Coal tits drop from leafless elm tree branch to one below, wait til that branch has stopped swaying, drop to lower one then fly back to top. / 8:22pm, Feb 19 2017: Owls called in the night woods as we searched for the lost keys, sweeping the ground with the torch that cast a green glow to the dog's eyes / 7:24pm, Feb 24 2017: Colder after the sun dropped; my pace guttering after my friend sped off: at the wood's edge jackdaws rose in a wave of haughty complaint. / 12:45pm, Feb 26 2017: Sea silvered then darkened, paw prints dampened steps; we leant against a raw clothes-tugging wind, the flag rope a percussion instrument. / 5:46pm, Mar 4 2017: I am the false herald of the Spring. Out in warm sun, back under slate sky, rushing wind and rain so cold my legs felt scalded. / 11:03am, Mar 3 2017: Stagger past dewponds 7, 8 & 9, fog condenses as chains of drips from trees, as fur to coat my clothes, as beads to make my glasses useless. / 1:33pm, Mar 11 2017: Fog very close on PoW-built path but on valley floor it lets more landscape in. Birds call from above cloud ceiling and behind fog curtain. / 8:11pm, Mar 17 2017: Morning's sun now a wind: to rattle pylon and fence: and blow crow down. / 11:22am, Mar 19 2017: After 10K, the banana's skin mottled a brown impression of my palm, its tips firm and cool, the centre the warm mush of childhood sandwiches / 12:39pm, Mar 25 2017: Butter-coloured butterfly flat to gravestone's warmth, budding branch clicks electric fence, drowsiness comes from sun and surf of traffic. / 2:12pm, Mar 25 2017: Its own composition: wind heaves off the ridge to set wires to whir, struts to rumble, loose signs to clatter and spaces between to whistle. / 4:57pm, Mar 27 2017: Standing at a suburban crossroads, I hear jackdaws "tchack" from the greening treetops and ten different birds forcing air as liquid rhythm. / 12:10pm, Apr 8 2017: Haze draws in and then recedes; wind picks up and then lets go. Encouraged by skylarks and acrobatic crows to forget heavy feet & sore knee / 1:12pm, Apr 8 2017: Just over half way – in distance if not in time – and my skin is salt, forehead wrinkled with the stuff. In the dappled cool of a copse now. / 2:45pm, Apr 8 2017: I am the stragglers' straggler, gait reduced to a shuffle, overtaken by ramblers, hurt but happy to be in this beauty. Nice chats help. / 5:46pm,

Apr 8 2017: Pheasant as rusty hinge, lamb as sound effect, digging deep into to my bag of secret mantras, for the powerful ones to get me to the end. / 3:44pm, Apr 21 2017: Footfalls crunched biscuity on paths parched craquelure, strewn with white blossom, bluebell hoods hanging, nettles reaching peak prickle. / 3:55pm, May 9 2017: Swifts swerved swarms of flies & skimmed pond, sipping water on go, rippling surface with rings. Crow hopped, dangling raw blood-fur carrion / 6:27pm, May 13 2017: Still warm to a finger-tip, its tail bent and hind-legs shattered, the shrew had been crushed just inches from the shelter of spring grasses / 2:33pm, May 14 2017: Watched gulls bob in rafts of spume and spray shoot off seawall; turned back to suddenly see city skyline recast for unoccupied investments / 10:04pm, May 22 2017: Lovely night run: Rorschach voids among trunks, shapes flaring from branches; sounds known and sounds unknown conspiring to load on the fear / 6:39am, May 25 2017: Heat high, horizon hazing sky and sea, magpie scolded as I near downed pigeon (blood where feathers plucked), sweat drips now onto keyboard. / 6:30pm, May 26 2017: Dusted with chalk, grained in salt, branded by sun; by the end, I wanted to dunk my searing head in the next filthy trough and drain it dry. / 10:12pm, May 30 2017: Acid tang of cow manure: a madeleine dipped in tea for memories of chilly stone floors, scratchy jumpers, cartoned milk and clouds of breath / 10:32pm, May 30 2017: Fearifying Night Run Sounds: 4. Distant shout: 3. Branch snap: 2. Sudden crash thru undergrowth: <drum roll>: 1. Discrete cough from darkness / 10:02pm, Jun 1 2017: Ten minutes to ten and the sun drags the last reds, purples and oranges down over the edge of the Downs. / 10:07pm, Jun 11 2017: Four moons for memory: amber, mauve, butter, silver; mist near is meadow blanket, mist far is whipped valley peaks; runners strung as stars. / 5:09pm, Jun 16 2017: Squirrels squawked in upper branches; Crickets crackled down below (each and every trill or throb tugged taut the aerial of my ears). / 3:45pm, Jun 18 2017: Sky burns my shoulders red and reflects sand in submarine yellows. Cormorants beat below hearing, oystercatchers pipe and join kids' shrieks / 8:23pm, Jun 23 2017: The path's freshest wild cherries shine firm, the earlier falls have darkened, softened, oozed and stained. Two fairy rings near the Beacon. / 10:23pm, Jul 4 2017: Not the burnt-out car I was after but owls launched across the meadow, crickets throbbed tired, branches snapped and this bug glowed green. / 1:45pm, Aug 29 2017: Four years into running through the South Downs, I come upon – just below a well-trodden trail – another zone, somewhere new to get lost in / 7:21pm, Sep 21 2017: Autumn is for running: puddled paths, grey skies darkening to evening, rotting litterfall, wet and bracing winds: joy / 2:45pm, Oct 8 2017: Running under mixed skies: ankles dusted with chalk then Pollocked by puddles; shoulders flecked with probably the last freckles of the year / 12:52pm, Oct 10 2017: The heron I startled – that startled me back – struggled to rise, trailing clawed legs to fly out of the gap in the canopy over the dew pond / 11:18am, Oct 12 2017: Morning dew pond, still rippling from the dog's leap that wrung a roar of anguish from its owner's mouth. Slight breeze sibilates the canopy / 3:07pm, Oct 15 2017: Two black bin bags as wind socks. One black bin bag as barbed-wire bunting. Finches fizzed, darted low, crows rode the wind, people happy.

Little Red Libraries

John Bevis

Driving through a Cambridgeshire village recently, I caught a glimpse of a red phone box partly filled with shelves of books. I knew about it, of course. This was the famous phone box library that had been in the national press a few years ago, with pictures, calling it the smallest library in the country, a telephone kiosk that, as far as I remembered, had been squatted by villagers and turned into a kind of pirate book exchange. I didn't recall it being in Cambridgeshire, but here it was.

Back home, I sought out the reports, which dated from 2009. It was not in Cambridgeshire after all, but at Westbury-sub-Mendip, which had to be in Somerset, and it was all above board. Residents had purchased the disused telephone box from BT, fitted it out with wooden shelves, and donated the books to fill them. It was free to all, and the intention was that books would be borrowed on a one-for-one exchange basis.

But then I found other headlines about similar enterprises, as if Westbury-sub-Mendip had never happened. Marton cum Grafton, North Yorkshire: "Villagers come up with novel idea for a phone box 'library'" (*Yorkshire Post*, 17 September 2010). Paxford, Gloucestershire: "Novel idea to turn phone box into a book library" (*Evesham Journal*, 4 October 2012). Kington Magna, Dorset: "What a novel idea—villagers transform redundant phone box into a library" (*Daily Express*, 11 September 2013). How many novel ideas for a phone box library were there?

The answer was, to my amazement, that in the UK in 2017 there are at least 160 red telephone box libraries. How had that happened? When I looked into it, I found the roots of the phenomenon went back to 2008, when BT disconnected many kiosks, particularly in rural areas, that were no longer considered cost effective. Some villages wanted to retain the iconic Giles Gilbert Scott designed K6 phone boxes, and in response to their petitions BT introduced the "Adopt a Kiosk" scheme, by which parish councils could take over the rights and responsibilities of their phone box for £1, while BT would continue to pay for the electricity used by the lights. Westbury-sub-Mendip had caught the headlines by being the first to be converted to a book exchange.

Strictly speaking they are not libraries. They don't function as lending libraries, as there is no membership roll, stock is not catalogued, there is no determined lending period and no facility for booking the loan of a particular title. There is some stock control, insofar as there is usually somebody charged with making an inventory from time to time, when any books that are sticking would be taken out and given to a charity shop. Otherwise, there is a strongly—attractively, some might argue—haphazard element to what is available for borrowing. It is questionable, too, whether they can be classed libraries under even the loosest use of the term, "a collection of publications", as there is nothing coherent, no sense of selection, of this being a collection. Nonetheless, while most are known as "book exchanges", or something similar—"book swap" or "book box" in some instances—around one-third are called, rightly or not, "libraries".

The distribution of these book exchanges across the map is a curious one. It is wildly uneven. They are a runaway success where it began, in Somerset, which has twenty-four at the time of writing, but the south-east counties, Surrey, Kent, and East and West Sussex, can muster only six between them. Cambridgeshire has a healthy thirteen, Oxfordshire only three. In the whole of Wales there are four, Scotland three, and Northern Ireland has none.

Where there are clusters, such as in Somerset, it may be that the scheme having worked for one village, neighbouring villages have followed suit. There is evidence that some book exchanges have come about as a result of the withdrawal or reduction of local mobile library provision, but there doesn't seem to be much correlation with the distance from a public library building. In fact, the provision seems unrelated to any obvious demographic such as wealth, age, class, literacy, mobility, religion or ethnicity. But it doesn't take much to piece together an image of the type of community where such a scheme might get off the ground: well-off enough to give books away, but pragmatic enough to recognise the value of a free read; the education to acquire a reading habit, and the leisure to maintain it; some common life experiences, reflected in common reading interests; a population small enough for its members to know each other, and stable enough for them to trust each other. A community of community-minded people; an Ambridge (almost: in BBC Radio 4's *The Archers*, the village phone box was adopted for use as a mini-information kiosk).

The main determining factor, though, is probably the opportunity presented by the Adopt a Kiosk scheme, although that does not answer why it is that while some kiosks are turned into book exchanges, others become art galleries, florists, tea and coffee houses, cake shops, souvenir shops, or mobile phone repair workshops. By far the least frivolous use, thanks to the efforts of the Community Heartbeat Trust, is as stations for defibrillators, which are now housed in more than 3,000 kiosks, often in tandem with some other function.

There are no phone cards, or library cards, to collect for telephone box libraries, of course. You can't use them to study or write in, or as a source of reference material. I don't feel the least inclination to go out of my way to visit some, or even a few of them. But I can't shake off the feeling that they are there, in some way, *to be done something with*.

Perhaps the answer is to make some sort of intervention, exchanging books so as to skew the contents of phone boxes libraries, spiking their shelves with unexpected titles? But what would that achieve? There is no mood for ironic subversion any more, or rather its hoarse old voice is inaudible in the current ethos of consensual anti-establishmentism, and the tracts of the old rebellious cultures, the Marxists, the druggists, the punks, feel so embraced by the mainstream that there is nothing daring to be done with them. Putting a book by Ginsberg or Kerouac in a phone box

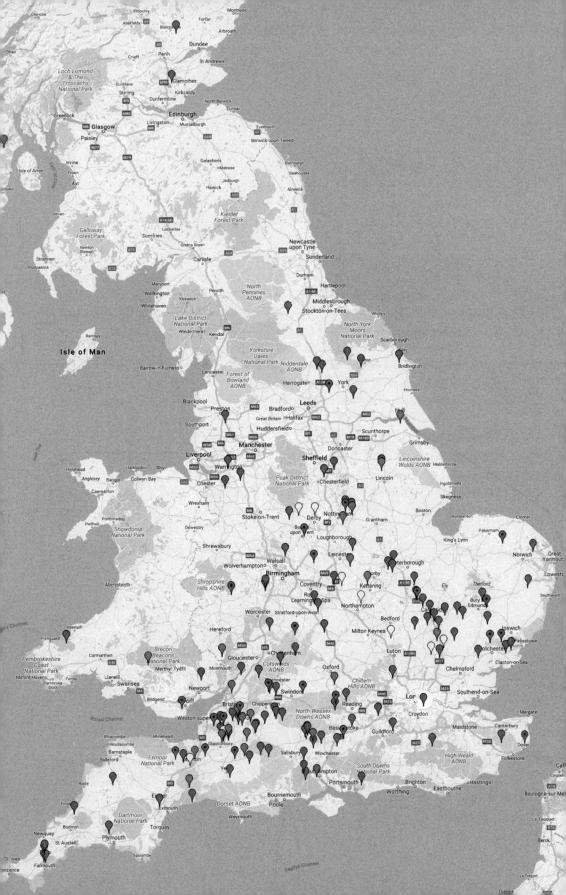

wouldn't raise the faintest blip on the cardiogram. There is also the feeling that I would be shooting myself in the foot if I were to gain a Danielle Steel for the loss of something as cherished as my copy of *Winnie the Pooh: Capitalist Lackey*.

But what might work would be something less blatant. The red phone box libraries have appeared in the aftermath of an iconic red, human-scale bookcase sculpture by Cardiff-based artist Peter Bailey. *The Little Red Library of Little Red Books* was a floor-standing wooden cabinet in the shape of an upright triangle, holding around one hundred books. The whole structure was painted lava red, and the books on its shelves were, well, small and red. As to being "little read", the pun on which the work revolved, I had assumed that this referred to their obscurity. In fact, checking the list of contents I find a share of best-sellers, and it appears more likely that the individual copies had qualified as little read on the basis that they had spent most of their lives unopened. *The Little Red Library* had been shown in 1981 at Coracle Press Gallery, in Camberwell New Road, London, where it could have been a totem for the gallery's print, book and object litany. Peter Bailey died in 2005, and I have no idea what came of his sculpture. But it had given me the germ of an idea.

My next opportunity to put this into practice was on a visit to Lichfield. Walking into town, the first place I came to that might have what I was after was an Oxfam bookshop. Much of the stock was newish paperbacks and unwanted-Christmas-present type hardbacks, but there was one narrow cabinet of older titles labelled "Interesting and collectible". I found myself drawn to a slim maroon spine, gilt embossed with the title *Wrecked*. The tale of a sailor, Ted Marshman, shipwrecked with his dog Dick on a remote island, the book was published in 1891 by Seeley & Co. The full title was *Wrecked, or, four years in a cave*, and the author was anonymous, credited simply as "By the author of 'Only a Dog'". There was a pink bookplate pasted into the front flyleaf identifying the book as having been a "Reward" presented to W. Lumby in 1899 by Leeds School Board for "Good Conduct, Proficiency & Regular Attendance". Gratifyingly, I have not been able to find out any more about the book in subsequent research, have found none of the original edition for sale, and feel confident that it is not only little and red, but also little read.

The plan was to search for copies of similar little red books, ones that Peter Bailey might have chosen himself from second-hand bookshops, junk shops or charity shops when assembling his collection of little red books, and place them in one of these more recent little red libraries. In exchange, for each red book I deposited I would remove a book that was not little—one that was taller or fatter than typical—and not red, and not little read, so something well thumbed, or an obvious bestseller. I visualised one of those great fat blockbuster paperbacks, its spine creased and incurved from having been plonked down with its pages open on sun loungers or patio decking.

In fact, I wouldn't have to make the switch many times over. One book on its own would do the trick, as I was working on a notionally broader project. According to Sheldrake's theorem, learned behaviour may be replicated without being copied. An example would be that if a blue tit learns to peck the cap of a milk bottle in, say, Somerset, then blue tits in Cambridgeshire or anywhere else in the country will be observed to exhibit the same behaviour, sooner or later. Sheldrake explains this as "morphic resonance", but whether this means some kind of mental osmosis, telepathy, or whether intelligence among blue tits is such a constant that any advance would inevitably peak not in an individual but across the population, I was not sure. But if the theorem held true, once I had placed my little red book in a little red library, before long similar events would begin to happen, and there would be, if not an explosion, then at least a perceptible increase in the occurrences of little red books in phone box libraries.

The following day, 28 September 2017, I had to be in Market Harborough, Leicestershire. I had checked my Google map of telephone box book exchanges, and discovered that there was one a few miles away. Burton Overy was everything I had anticipated, a trim, affluent community of Georgian red-brick cottages, scattered daintily around the essential hub of pub, church and village hall. I'd expected the kiosk to be part of that axis, but found it tucked away to the edge of the village, half-hidden in an avenue of trees, perhaps deliberately out of earshot. On the outside it was unchanged from its previous incarnation, and there was no notice or sign to give a title or explanation to its new purpose. Unchanged, but different, and it took me a while to realise that its many glass panes were spotlessly clean.

Stepping inside, I braced myself for the customary eau-de-kiosk, unnecessarily since for the first time in my life I experienced a telephone box sanitised with something other than Jeyes Fluid. There were five shelves, filled to overflowing with about the same number of books as the *Little Red Library* or perhaps a few more, I would estimate maybe 150 books. They were much of a muchness with the general stock of the Lichfield Oxfam bookshop, holiday novels, bestsellers, and a few hardback non-fiction titles including books on the Romanovs, Queen Victoria & Prince Albert, and Eric Sykes. There was just space on the shelf for my copy of *Wrecked*, antique in its prayer-book binding, a sombre note among the gaudy thrillers. I hoped somebody would want it.

I had already gone off the idea of taking in exchange anything with no apparent merit, anything I wouldn't wish on anybody else. With all these spines looking so similar and to my eyes uninviting, I was at a loss to know how to make a choice. I was about to shut my eyes and pick a book at random, when I spotted the perfect title. *The Book Thief*, by Markus Zusak. I put it in my bag, took a few photos, and got back in my car.

The next step would be for me to place *The Book Thief* on the shelf of another kiosk library. Sheldrake's theorem would see to it that books would then be borrowed from one little library and returned to another, across the country. I recognise that this is a robust test of the theorem, as most borrowing and returning would surely be from and to the same place, this being an insular community activity. But once *The Book Thief* and I had started the trend, the little red world would follow. What would result, if Rupert Sheldrake was right, was that some of the increasing number of little red books appearing at random in telephone kiosks would be exchanged to other kiosks, allowing the possibility that in time someone, somewhere, would find themselves driving past a phone box, just as I had driven past the one in Cambridgeshire, and would notice that it was full of little red books, a modest and arbitrary homage to Peter Bailey and his *Little Red Library of Little Red Books*.

The following week I was back in Lichfield, where I found myself within a couple of miles of one of the very few telephone box book exchanges in the West Midlands, at Wall in Staffordshire ("Novel idea as villagers convert red phone box into library", *Belfast Telegraph*, 10 November 2015). I was pleased at the symmetry of completing the project so close to where it had begun, of the book exchange being geographic too. But the phone box at Wall was glassless and wrapped in security tape, a notice on the door informing that it was closed for re-glazing and painting.

For a couple of weeks I carried *The Book Thief* in my bag, ready for the next opportunity. I didn't have long to wait: I was due to visit Uttoxeter, where just a few miles away, across the Derbyshire border, was the plausible-sounding Marston Montgomery, complete with kiosk book-exchange. But there was something random and out-of-the-loop about its location, a feeling that it didn't connect to my little project. Wall, on the other hand, was not only proximate to Lichfield, but its phone box was on the pavement of Watling Street. On a personal level this carried weight, as the highway's start and finish, in London and Wroxeter, were close to the two places that my life pivots between; more potently, the Roman artery stood as symbol of connectedness for its millennium, as much as the red phone box for the twentieth century. I decided to wait for the restoration of the Wall phone-box library.

Hearings

Cathy Lane

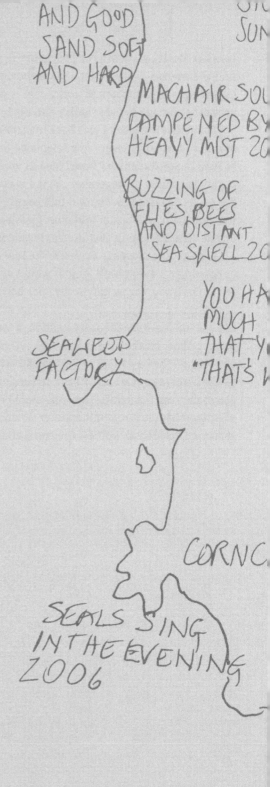

What is landscape but a map of activity past and present?

Places hold and anchor memories as much as archives. Over the last decade the Outer Hebrides off the west coast of Scotland have been the focus of much of my work. Through interviews, field recordings and existing oral history materials I have been investigating aspects of people's relationship to place, trying to move beyond the visual and to listen out for the sonic traces of past lives and past events. These listenings, often conducted in collaboration with local residents, have involved landscape, language, song, stories, music, weather, labour, religion and culture.

HUM OF FRIDGE,
BLEEP, KERCHINK 2008

WE USED TO GO IN A
WRITE OUR NAMES ON
THE DRIVE

QUAVERS

I LIKE GOING TO
LOCH BOISDALE

RODDY'S ROAD AFTER
MY GRANDPA

BIG

NKSO
OL
T WALK
OK THE CAR

MARGARET
LISTENING A

CHURCH WITH
LONG ECHO 2006

2006

STATION HUM 2008
GENERATOR
HUM 2006

BIRDS
EVERYWHE

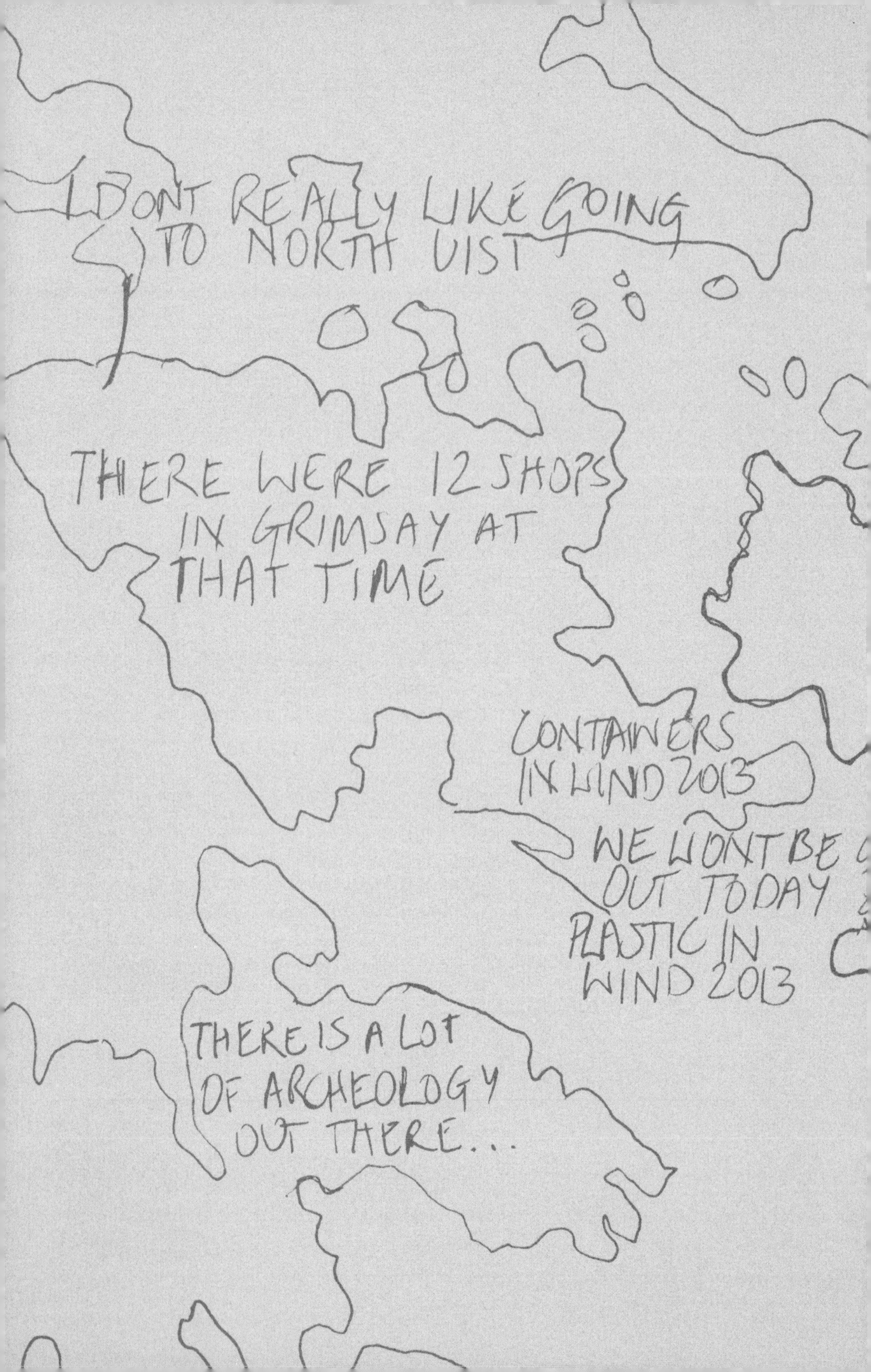

I DONT REALLY LIKE GOING
TO NORTH UIST

THERE WERE 12 SHOPS
IN GRIMSAY AT
THAT TIME

CONTAINERS
IN WIND 2013

WE WONT BE
OUT TODAY
PLASTIC IN
WIND 2013

THERE IS A LOT
OF ARCHEOLOGY
OUT THERE...

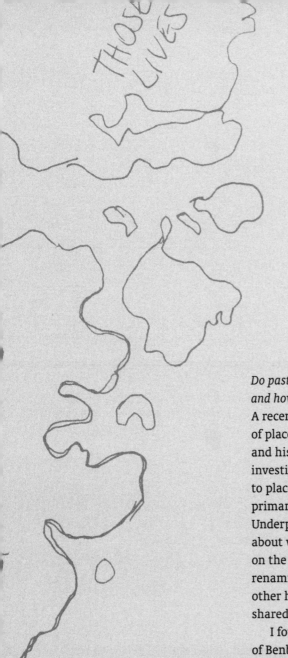

*Do past lives and past events leave sonic traces
and how can we hear them in the present?*
A recent project focused on the 'resonances'
of place names and how they 'fix' memories
and historical events onto a landscape. It also
investigated intergenerational relationships
to place names through the medium of sound,
primarily oral history recordings old and new.
Underpinning this research were questions
about whose history could be commemorated
on the landscape with the aim of anecdotally
renaming some of these places according to
other histories and other memories, both
shared and individual.

I found that for the crofting communities
of Benbecula, North and South Uist the land
holds individualised yet shared memories of
place and function. Place names, particularly
those in Gaelic, act as a mnemonic for a
dynamic memory re-creation. It is as if a
mesh of past, present, ideas of kinship, place,
features of the landscape and the shared
and personal experiences of each speaker
and listener covers and overlays the lived
landscape.

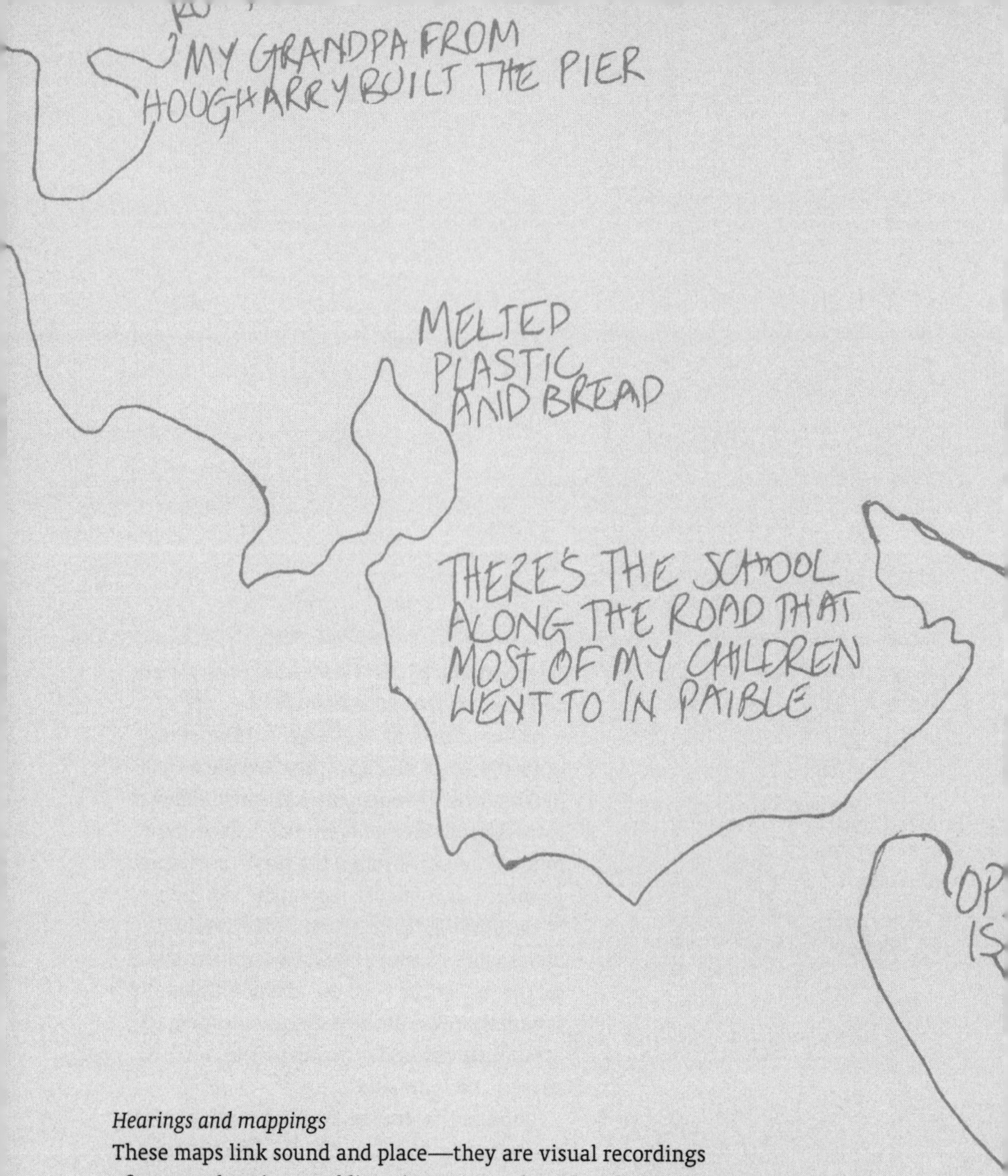

MY GRANDPA FROM
HOUGHARRY BUILT THE PIER

MELTED
PLASTIC
AND BREAD

THERE'S THE SCHOOL
ALONG THE ROAD THAT
MOST OF MY CHILDREN
WENT TO IN PAIBLE

OP
IS

Hearings and mappings
These maps link sound and place—they are visual recordings
of my past hearings and listenings, some shared with others,
some experienced alone, as well as the places heard about from
listening to other people recounting episodes in their own
personal histories and those of their ancestors, often going back
several generations. As we move over and through a landscape
we reactivate these traces which only exist as a fleeting memory
of sounds heard. These and the located memories of others,
recorded verbatim, cover and overlay the maps revealing the
shared and personal experiences of the speakers and listener.

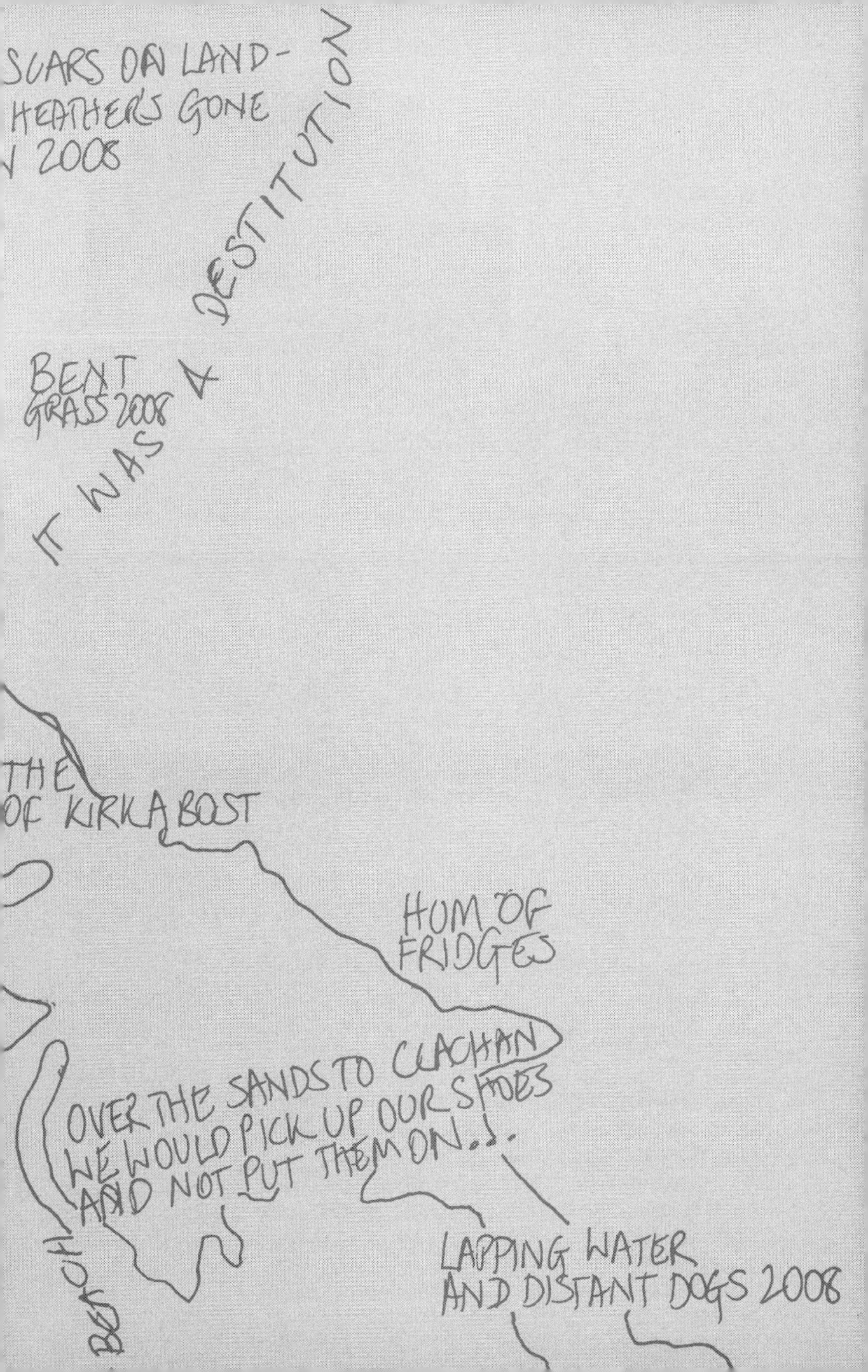

SCARS ON LAND—
HEATHER'S GONE
2008

DESTITUTION

BENT
GRASS 2008

IT WAS A

THE
OF KIRKABOST

HUM OF
FRIDGES

OVER THE SANDS TO CLACHAN
WE WOULD PICK UP OUR SHOES
AND NOT PUT THEM ON...

BEACH

LAPPING WATER
AND DISTANT DOGS 2008

POV: Co-ordinate checks, cat's cradles, wayside halts, photo opportunities, a catalogue of local impressions, pub grub. Walking is structured cognitively around observation as much as forward motion: namely that which snags your attention in the street, landscape, or blurs against the horizon.—Michael Hampton in front of a view protected by the Richmond, Ham and Petersham Open Spaces Act, 1902; photograph by Ailsa Ferrier, Christmas 2013.

GREAT
CHOIR
4 CLARION
8 TRUMPET
TREMULANT
MIXTURE
8 CORNO DI BASSETTO
2 PICCOLO
2 FIFTEENTH
3 TWELFTH
4 LIEBLICH FLOTE
4 PRINCIPAL
4 CONCERT FLUTE
4 FLUTE HARMONIQUE
8 CLARIBEL FLUTE
8 CLARIBEL FLUTE
8 LIEBLICH GEDACT
8 STOPPED DIAPASON
8 DULCIANA
8 FLAUTO DOLCE
8 VIOL D'AMORE
8 OPEN DIAPASON
16 DOUBLE OPEN DIAPASON

Swell Engine

Dawn Scarfe

I listened to a water tower in Norfolk whistling in a gale. I was drawn to the fluctuating mix of mournful aeolian tones in the wake eddies of the chimney, and the unsettling roar that rattled down the flue with the strongest gusts. I made a sound recording in the tower's draughty spiral stairwell.

Some time later I was trying to modify the sound of small speakers by putting them in boxes, and used the stairwell recording as a test file. It struck me that this was perverse thing to do for a couple of reasons: confining sound in general, and placing a windy 'outside' sound inside a container. Lifting the lid of the box unleashed the sound, like opening the door of a stove, or yawning.

In Summer 2017 Claire Singer gave me a tour of the Henry Willis Organ at Union Chapel. Of all the characteristics of the huge instrument: the electric and hydraulic blowing engines; the array of curiously named stops (Tremulant, Mixture, Lieblich Gedact...); the swell mechanism intrigued me the most. I was initially taken by the connotations of sea swell, then the idea of engineering an effect associated with the accumulation of fluid or the welling of feeling.

I learned that swell boxes were added to organs to perform an expressive function which they had previously lacked. Organ pipes were enclosed in a cabinet with shutters. A closed box made the sound feel muted and distant. Gradually opening or closing the shutters either 'swelled' or attenuated the sound. In the early eighteenth century master organ builder Renatus Harris explained that the swell mechanism should operate in a smooth manner, uninterrupted by steps in the apparatus "as if inspir'd by the human breath".

Claire asked me to make an installation for the 'Organ Reframed' festival at Union Chapel, to be located in the "stony stairwell". The highest flight of stairs got increasingly obscure with decreasing headroom, less light, and a small padlocked door at the top which opened out to the roof. It was marked by a paper sign which seemed to indicate that a "universal stone" could be found at the top. This narrow space had a distinctive acoustic, all the hard reflective surfaces lengthened and changed the character of sounds passing through.

It seemed to make sense to respond to the brief by drawing on the mechanical processes at work in the organ. I turned to Thomas Eisl who has an intuitive grasp on the inner workings of machines, hoping we might collaborate. After discussing cams, compressors and pneumatic disc breaks on London buses, and practical experiments with bellows and bicycle inner tubes, I returned to the 'wind in a box' experience. I wondered if this could be applied to a series self-opening 'swell' boxes. Within a few days, Thomas contrived a lid opening mechanism driven by motors from dismembered CCTV cameras. Fortuitously, running off 12 volt batteries, the motors delivered a smooth pace, allowing the lids to rise and fall at a similar rate to relaxed breathing. We aimed for four different boxes. Variations in the design and weight of each lid led to non-synchronised opening–closing action. We agreed that the boxes should be placed on the stairs in a casual, 'left behind' kind of way.

I tried playing a number of windy recordings through the boxes, including the water tower in Norfolk and an exposed bird hide on dunes at South Walney (looking out towards some of the world's biggest offshore wind farms). But these proved too varied to work in the swell boxes, distracting from the acoustic effects of the lids opening and closing. So, instead, I made a mix of brown and pink noise, the signal patterns of which resemble the random movement of particles in liquid, and the rise and fall of the tide respectively. These were in turn filtered by the lo-fi quality of the speakers, the materials and dimensions of each box, the moving lids, and the 'voice' of the stony stairwell.

Swell Engine, with Thomas Eisl, 2017; commissioned by 'Organ Reframed', Union Chapel, London. Still from: vimeo.com/238177108

Contributors

The title-page and cover drawing is 'Measurement with a pencil held at arm's length' by Geoffrey Hutchings, from his booklet *An Introduction to Geographical Landscape Drawing*, 1955.

John Bevis is a writer specialising in nature and the arts, poetry and criticism. His definitive study of the pioneering early photographers *The Keartons: inventing nature photography* was published by Uniformbooks in 2016.

Peter Blegvad is a songwriter, graphic artist, writer and broadcaster. In 2014, Uniformbooks published *Kew. Rhone.*, a thorough excavation of the visual and lyrical themes and sources within this categorically elusive album, first released in 1977.

Kevin Boniface, artist, writer, postman, lives and works in Huddersfield, West Yorkshire. Uniformbooks will be publishing an as-yet-untitled collection of his local writings and photographs in 2018.

Janet Boulton is a painter of still-life, as well as of gardens. The various aspects of her work, the watercolours and paper reliefs made since the late 1970s, are examined in the new publication: *A Seeming Diversity: Painting & Reliefs*.

Angus Carlyle is an academic, artist, writer, slow runner, and interested in landscape. Uniformbooks published his *A Downland Index* in 2016, and earlier, *In the Field: The Art of Field Recording* and *On Listening*, both in collaboration with Cathy Lane.

J. R. Carpenter is an artist, writer, performer, and independent researcher working in the intersecting fields of performance writing, digital literature, and media archaeology. Her hybrid web/print work *The Gathering Cloud* was published by Uniformbooks in 2017.

Rebecca Chesney is interested in how we perceive land: how we romanticise, translate and define urban and rural spaces. She looks at how politics, ownership, management and commercial value all influence our surroundings, and has made extensive investigations into the impact of human activities on nature and the environment.

Les Coleman, who died in 2013, was an artist, writer, publisher, lecturer, critic, and collector. Alongside these various activities, he was an explorer of the surreal, obscure and esoteric, and accumulated a unique and significant literary and visual archive.

Simon Cutts is a poet, artist, and editor, who has developed Coracle Press over the last forty years in its many publicational forms. His own concern is with the book and it's mechanisms as a manifestation of the poem itself. Uniformbooks published his *Letterpress: New and material poems* in 2013.

Caitlin DeSilvey is associate professor of cultural geography at the University of Exeter, she was co-editor of the first Uniformbooks title *Anticipatory history* as well as co-author of *Visible mending: Everyday repairs in the South West*. Her monograph *Curated Decay: Heritage Beyond Saving* was published in 2017.

Michael Hampton is a writer and critic who has contributed to numerous magazines, journals and catalogues, writing regularly for *Art Monthly*. In 2015 Uniformbooks published his revisionist history *Unshelfmarked: Reconceiving the artists' book*.

Matthew Kelly is professor of modern history at the University of Northumbria. His work focusses on the development of environmental policy in the postwar period and the cultural history of landscape. He is author of *Quartz and Feldspar: A History of Modern Dartmoor*.

Cathy Lane is a sound artist and academic. Her work uses spoken word, field recordings and archive material. Books include *Playing with Words: The Spoken Word in Artistic Practice* (2008) and, with Angus Carlyle, *In the Field* and *On Listening* (both 2013). Her CD *The Hebrides Suite* was released in 2013.

Brian Lewis is the editor and publisher of Longbarrow Press, a Sheffield-based collective that supports and develops collaborations between poets and artists. He is also an essayist and poet, his recent publications include *East Wind* and *White Thorns*.

Phil Owen is a writer and singer based in Bristol. He set up Tertulia with Megan Wakefield, a salon event for people interested in voice and language. His piece 'Estuary' was published in *Uniformagazine* no.9.

Colin Sackett's self-published work since the 1980s has been an investigation of editing and content, the licence to take broad issue and to play with the form, both disruptively and demonstrably. He is editor and publisher of Uniformbooks and *Uniformagazine*.

Dawn Scarfe is an artist whose work investigates resonance, perception and environmental atmospheres. She works across a variety of media and contexts including site-specific installation, performance and field recording.

Tim Staples is an occasional artist who lives and works in Bristol. He grew up on a farm in Worcestershire before attending Exeter College of Art in the late 1970s. He has made exhibitions, publications, and taught in art schools.

Gertrude Stein's *Tender Buttons*, written in 1912, was republished a century later by Uniformbooks in a newly formatted edition. As with 'Geography' printed here, conventionally indented paragraphs are reset as if prose-poetry, liberating the reading from the conventions of narrative text.

Erica Van Horn is an artist, writer, printer, and book maker. *Living Locally* was published by Uniformbooks in 2014, gathering entries from her daily journal where she writes about rural life in and around a farming valley in Tipperary, Ireland.

Ian Waites's research is concerned with the landscapes, histories, dreams and memories of postwar England. His recollective work about his childhood environment, *Middlefield: A postwar council estate in time* was published by Uniformbooks in 2017.

Nathan Walker's work constructs relationships between performance and writing. Uniformbooks published his *Condensations* in 2017: slow-collage-word-terrains, resulting from a residency at the Armitt Museum in Cumbria.

Tom Wilkinson is a photographer of landscapes, who also explores and writes about the nature of philosophical ideas in photography. His first Google Landscapes were published in *Uniformagazine* no.6.

Ken Worpole is a writer and social historian, whose work includes architecture, landscape and contemporary culture. He has recently collaborated on the book *The New English Landscape* with photographer Jason Orton, exploring the value and meaning of place.

Uniformbooks

Titles 2011–2017

Anticipatory history

Wordage
Colin Sackett

Tender Buttons
Gertrude Stein

In the Field
The Art of Field Recording
Cathy Lane & Angus Carlyle

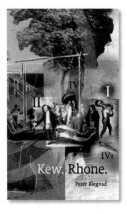

Kew. Rhone.
Peter Blegvad

The Book of the Green Man
Ronald Johnson

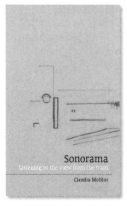

Sonorama
Listening to the view from the train
Claudia Molitor

Unshelfmarked
Reconceiving the artists' book

A Downland Index
Angus Carlyle

Modern Futures
Edited by Hannah Neate & Ruth Craggs

All or nothing
and other pages
Michael Gibbs

Condensations
Nathan Walker